IT'S ABOUT TIME

IT'S ABOUT TIME

GREAT RECIPES FOR EVERYDAY LIFE

Michael Schlow

Photography by Shimon and Tammar

STEERFORTH PRESS
HANOVER, NEW HAMPSHIRE

It's About Time

Michael Schlow

Steerforth Press
Hanover, New Hampshire
Copyright © 2005 by Michael Schlow

For information about permission to reproduce
selections from this book, write to:
Steerforth Press L.C., 25 Lebanon Street,
Hanover, New Hampshire 03755

Photography by Shimon & Tammar
Prop styling by Marina Malchin
Food styling by Liza Jernow
Book design by Louise Fili & Chad Roberts / Louise Fili Ltd
Design assistance by Courtney Waddell

Library of Congress Cataloging-in-Publication Data

Schlow, Michael.
   It's about time : great recipes for everyday life / Michael Schlow ;
foreword by Mario Batali ; photographs by Shimon and Tammar.— 1st ed.
       p. cm.
   Includes index.
   ISBN 1-58642-087-9 (alk. paper) 1. Cookery. I. Title.

   TX714.S34 2005 641.5—dc22 2004026414

FIRST EDITION

ACKNOWLEDGMENTS

This book is dedicated to my parents, Ned and Judy.
Your constant love, support, advice, and encouragement are what make everything seem possible to me.
Words can never fully express my appreciation and love for you.

An extraordinary amount of communication and understanding is necessary to have a successful relationship, whether it is business or personal. Nothing I say can truly describe how indebted I am to my two closest friends and business partners, Christopher Myers and Esti Parsons. In addition to their day jobs, they also act as my teachers, psychiatrists, cheerleaders, protectors, conscience.... I could not ask for better surroundings. Thanks for always keeping *everyone's* best interests at heart.

Special thank you and love to my best friend from childhood, Zoub. You get your very own line, since you've always been in a league of your own.

The real "foodies" in my life are my family, and the herd is constantly growing. Robert (RSchlow) and Sue, Risa and Andrew, Lisa, Rachel, Jack, Zoe, Noah, Joshua, Zachary, Ann, Ruthie and Sol, Albie, David and Kara, Larry and Gina, Mark and Maryanne, Tom and Shari — you are all such an essential part of my life. Your understanding and compassion about hectic schedules and missed holidays is nothing short of miraculous. Thank you, thank you.

Special *grazie mille* to Mario Batali, for not only writing a foreword that could make a man blush, but for understanding the true definition of friendship. Now if we can only straighten out that nasty slice of yours....

I owe special thank yous to different people from different walks of life; they have all had an impact on my life. In no particular order, thank you to: Alesandro and all the Zeccas, Jeremy Sewall, Peter Wolf, Susan and Malcolm, The Noodle, Jimmy P., Billy Joel and Kate Lee, Brian Reimer, Luis Morales, Jack and Suzy Welch, Darimichele, Cam and Paulina Neely, Michael Rossi, Sheila Bossier, Griff, everyone at the Hotel Commonwealth, Gabriel Frasca, Jules, MED, June Mariani, Peej, Nick, 'Styna, Scott, Marco, Lee, Guy Neal, Kerry Lynch, and all of the staffs, front and back, as well as all of the investors, of Radius, Via Matta, and Great Bay, Jay and Penny, Kirk and Mary (and everyone at Perona), Paul and Donnie, Suzanne and David, Gabrielle Hamilton, Craig and Isabelle Shelton, Joe Bastianich, el Willie, Takashi, Eric and Vicki, Ike, Lim, Ming, Kenny, Super J, Michael Ginor, Mark Strausman, Seth and Angela from The Pearl, Marc Orfaly, Jasper White, Paul Connors, Burke and Jill "Bomb" Forester, Joho, and the entire Boston restaurant scene — you make the culinary world a better place. I have learned from and thank you all.

Shimon and Tammar Rothstein, the incredibly talented photographers, thank you for your vision and ability to find beauty in the most unlikely of places.

Thank you to food stylist Liza Jernow and prop stylist Marina Malchin for making my food look better than ever.

Louise Fili and Chad Roberts. Simply put, this book would not exist without you. Thank you for your taste, style, and incredible listening skills.

Larry Moulter from the Helen Rees Agency, my friend and literary agent (how many times are those words used in the same sentence?), thank you for fighting all of my battles and representing my best interests with grace and professionalism. I'm lucky to have you on my team!

Scott Feldman and everyone at (112?), no, two twelve management. Thanks doesn't even start to say it.

Stuart Horowitz and Rudy Vale from Entity — a special thank you for taking this book from its earliest days and thoughts and turning into something we can all be proud of. You both spent so much time and energy on this project — from the bottom of my heart, thank you.

Teresa Lust and Kristin Sperber for editing my crazy ramblings and horrific grammar.

Finally, and perhaps most importantly, a giant thank you to Chip Fleischer and everyone at Steerforth Press. Thank you for your vision, faith, countless hours, helping me find my voice, and for letting me write the book I wanted to write. Thank you!

Michael Schlow was the first American cook I ever saw turn the oven down. Way down. All the other restaurant chefs I had ever worked with in America always beseeched me, along with the rest of their kitchen associates, as well as the very ovens and stoves themselves, to do just the opposite: Cook faster and harder, higher and hotter and more intensely; an oven simply could not be turned up high enough.

At Radius in the fall of 1999, Michael, his team, and I were prepping for a dinner that would take place the following night; the occasion was to celebrate and promote my latest cookbook. Naturally, as all my past experiences led me to believe, I expected nothing but intensely hot ovens.

As I observed the chefs in the kitchen the night before the big dinner, I noticed the ovens were turned to 300°F or lower. This is slow for baking brownies, slow even for home cooks. It is the temperature of Easy-Bake Ovens and the rest of their 125-watt ilk, I thought. And I was chuckling softly at such folly when I tasted a bite of Michael's lamb, an end-piece trimmed away for a more elegant presentation on the plate.

It was poetry, and that night in the kitchen at Radius I watched and I learned.

Michael's practice of slow cooking — roasting and sautéing at low temperatures — allows the interior of his cuts of lamb, beef, duck, or any meat for that matter, to cook more evenly through to the center. Admirable? Yes. Efficient? Hardly. Not to mention impossible for a restaurant, or so the lore would lead us to believe! His technique was not actually revolutionary; I had heard of Alain Passard cooking an entire leg of lamb in a sauté pan on the burners at Arpege in Paris. And I had always admired Crock-Pots and the type of granny-driven cooking Tom Valenti had been living and breathing for a decade at his restaurants in New York City. But things were different at Radius. Michael's food at Radius had a range of flavors and textures unlike anything I'd been making or tasting all those years, and I was swept away by it. As for the book dinner the following night, it went even better than I expected — the team at Radius seemed motivated by a higher order, even though I had their precious cold ovens turned up to a hell-rattling 525°F.

Mr. Schlow employs this slow-cooking technique in all his restaurants, and I have been a big fan of everything he has shown me ever since: his whimsical take on Modern French cooking at Radius, his ode to the cuisine of the Italian countryside at Via Matta, his reinterpretation of Yankee seafood at Great Bay. So I shouldn't have been surprised, then, when he told me about his idea for a cookbook. Still, the man has three big-shot restaurants to run and hordes of food writers to impress. I assumed he would churn out the media-savvy überchef's requisite business card — a culinary opus in four-color fantasy to showcase a collection of a hundred recipes calling for hard-to-find ingredients and a team of twelve to spend the day in the kitchen making stocks and chopping vegetables into origami.

Instead Michael said he wanted to write a book about cookery and time. I understood time with respect to baking cakes, and time lapsed in regard to freshness, or thyme as a flavoring for white beans and garlic. Even beer-time at the end of a shift in a hot kitchen. But time itself?

Yet time is so often the most important factor in determining what one cooks, nay, even whether one cooks at all. Time is equal for all: no one has enough of it, and while there is constant pressure to get by with less, we all need to remember to make more. So of course Michael Schlow, who insists on stretching and folding time to fit slow cooking into the frenetic pace of a restaurant sauté line, would approach his cookbook from the perspective of this most precious resource. Time is why people will buy this book. It is the reason they will find themselves cooking not only from it, but with it, through it, and because of it.

The recipes herein represent the best of what the chefs of my generation are doing — all the modern stuff we have been taught to think and say in our quirky and publicist-ready soundbites for the national shows. But Michael's cooking is distinctively and deliciously his own, and his recipes reflect that.

His approach makes sense, and it makes for better tasting food. So, even under pressure from big-time New York City line cooks, some of my ovens will remain turned down as well. And I like that.

AN INTRODUCTION TO MICHAEL SCHLOW

Christopher Myers

I'm sitting at a restaurant in the Chelsea neighborhood of New York City. It's a new place, off to a torrid start after a surprise three-star review in the *Times*. My girlfriend and I are thrilled to be here; our food trips to the city not nearly as easy to pull off as they once were. I'm particularly tickled this evening, because the bartender taking care of us is a former employee of mine. Or, more accurately, of ours. Scottie was the BBOC (big bartender on campus) of our opening staff at Radius, the first restaurant that I opened with my closest friends, Esti Parsons and Chef Michael Schlow. It's an exquisite privilege to watch someone that we trained, possibly even inspired, give great service in a successful New York restaurant. This place is humming, the food righteous, the cocktails cold, and the service excellent. Scott works the bar like he's enjoying himself as much as his guests, a wonderful sight in any restaurant. He's taking care of everyone; it's a great dance hall and he's leading each guest through the Byzantine steps.

The night rolls along and Scott, Joanne, and I are sharing a curiosity about a friend none of us has seen in awhile when, out of the blue, a sweet, doe-eyed stranger on my right asks us a question. Then another. She's been eavesdropping and before we know it, she announces that she grew up with Michael Schlow, that she's known him forever, that she's still friends with his sister, and on and on. What else I wonder? Almost immediately I begin my customary inquiry, hoping to discover something she knows about MSchlow, something I can work with in the future. Perhaps that Chef Michael Schlow, winner of the James Beard Award for Best Chef in the Northeast, in his first year of eligibility no less, was lead flute in the high-school band, or better yet, alto soprano in the Glee Club. Or, better even still, that he played Puck in lime-green pantyhose in his senior play! I want pictures!!!

We're exchanging niceties and this lovely lady, now "Dr." Sweet Doe-Eyed Stranger, is in full form. She's got a cocktail going and she's flooding us with a tidal wave of stories about Michael's entire family. This is going to be good. My imagination swims; surely there is an arrest in there somewhere. Dare I wish for hard-time served? I'm beside myself as I imagine cutting and pasting his post office mug shot into our employee newsletter! And then, in an instant, the entire conversation turns on a dime. The Doctor offers an observation that doesn't so much spoil my fun as reaffirm why I have so much fun in life, every day. Rather than leaving us with scandalous tidbits to torch the nerve endings of my best friend upon my return to Boston, what Dr. Sweet Doe-Eyed Stranger remembers most vividly about my boy, about MSchlow, is that "he threw great parties, the best parties in Somerville, New Jersey. Even in junior high, he loved to throw a party."

I embrace this with some disappointment before I take a moment and realize that I'm actually amused by this, all of this. I'm amused by the coincidences, the collision of friends, strangers, and former colleagues, all above the squeaky bonhomie of diners straining over the music. I'm amused by the alcohol, certainly, but mostly I'm amused by the right-on-the-money characterization of Michael Schlow.

It is by no means rare for me to meet someone who is aware of Michael, someone who has heard of him, someone who has eaten his food, downloaded his menus off the Radius Web site, met him at some fundraiser that he's given his time to, some schoolmate from culinary school, who worked with him at Sapore di Mare in the eighties, at the Ryland Inn or Le Madri in the nineties, ate his food at Via Matta "and damn near *plotzed*, it was so Italian! And you're Jewish? Single?" No industry throws a wider net than the food industry. It's part of its infinite appeal. But to meet someone that knows him, *really knows* him, *knows* the inner Schlow, the *raison d'Schlow*, this is a rare occurrence. And far from finding out something I don't know, Dr. Sweet Doe-Eyed Stranger has confirmed exactly what I do know. Michael hasn't changed a bit since junior high, for crying out loud. He acquired a massive stockpot of talent along the way, for sure, but damn if he's not the same kid at forty that he was at fifteen! The man just loves to throw a party, go to a party, crash a party.

When Michael and I got together to go into business, we made a lot of promises to each other. Reflecting on those promises, on all those meetings, we were shooting high, thinking out of the box and into the heavens. Nothing was going to stop us. Esti Parsons, Michael, and myself, we were going to open what we hoped would be one of the most exciting new restaurants in the country. We talked and rambled into many a night about the hard work that lay ahead, the long days and longer nights. We fully realized that we weren't going to see a beach, or a sunset, or the sun for that matter, for probably another five years. We would inevitably watch our relationships fall apart. That's what a new restaurant does to the innocent; we would emerge from the experience, mere shells of our former happy selves. We would watch our Levi sizes expand, and shrink, and expand again. But we'd be happy, right? During one particularly inspired meeting, I vividly recall Michael crystallizing what our lives were going to be about. He said that no matter how hard the work would be, ultimately, "We're going to throw a party every single night of our lives. That's how we'll train our staffs, how we'll go about our business, how we'll view our existence. And what better way to spend a life than that." What better way?

Chefs spend the better years of their apprenticeship talking to themselves, to other chefs, to kumquats and sweetbreads, to microgreens and reductions. The rest of the time they're yelling. The result of this is that most chefs develop their culinary skills long before their personalities. This can be a problem in today's world, as we now expect our chefs to show their faces, to mingle in the dining room, to spread charm and hospitality as smooth as a mousseline. But when your finishing school is a professional kitchen, a place where idle chat is as welcome as a Jersey tomato in December, miracles of personality seldom occur.

MSchlow, as I call him, is a different sort of chef. How he kept his mouth shut during culinary school is still a mystery to me. Working with the feisty Pino Luongo and the feistier Mark Straussman must have been a Herculean challenge. Talking back to that pair is none too healthy behavior. Yet for all his restraint in those early years, and for all his culinary ability, he's emerged far more gifted, spreading more bright cheer and goodwill than most of the hosts, managers, and maître d's that I've had the pleasure of working with over my years in the business. He loves the entire experience, the whole enjoyable, convivial artistry of the dining room. In short, he's a chef who is out in the dining room not to market his new book, not for the egoism of getting the praise and idolatry that can come with the position, with the "evil power of the white coat" as I've been known to call it. He's in the dining room to share in the enjoyment of his guests, to watch as they cut into a brightly colored squab breast. And heaven help us all if it's not cooked "on the money." To borrow an expression from my mother, Michael can be "as subtle as an air raid" when things aren't perfect. He'll burrow his head right into your plate to make sure that your golden pintade is cooked perfectly. He'll steal the fork from between your fingers and the knife from betwixt your hands before he'll allow you to eat something that he doesn't feel is the best he can offer. He's a hospitality provider before all else.

Knowing what I know about Schlow's gregarious and bountiful nature, after years of friendship and eight years as business partners, I should have anticipated the brawls that lay ahead when we discussed the direction and flavor of this cookbook. I wanted "our" book to be utter Hollywood, the big-shot, Technicolor, celebrity collector's item. After all, I've got a million of them; I've forked out the cash for so many luscious, downright pornographic food pictorials and, not being much of a home cook, I was convinced that cookbooks were for looking and not for cooking. Each time I attempted a meal from these celebrity tomes, these gifts from the culinary magi, I always ended up eternally grateful that if I didn't have the talent to execute these mind-boggling, time-robbing recipes, at least I possessed the wisdom to live a mere block and a half from Chinatown.

From time to time my limited skill set was rescued by the rare cookbook, written by the equally rare chef, and even I managed to pull off the unthinkable: an edible dish prepared in my very own kitchen! Praise be to Mario Batali, Tom Colicchio, and Lidia Bastianich, and all hail to those gods swimming in my local waters but teaching like understanding, avenging angels — Chris Schlesinger, Gordon Hamersley, and Jasper White. And Julia, ahhh, Julia. The kitchen accursed can always find refuge and a reliable repast in Julia.

But reliability and pragmatism be damned, the full-blown *Cook's Illustrated* pictorial was the way to go, it made business sense, it was good for Radius, and it was the savvy, big-city strategy. Maybe Francesco Scavullo could do the photography, he's still alive, isn't he? Giselle could hold each dish! I wanted this book in the guests' constant view, a token of your civilization, a soft-spoken but hard-to-miss road sign that points your neighbors and friends in the direction of your lofty good taste in food, in restaurants, in the company you keep. I wanted our book to sit out on coffee tables, boastfully, glistening forever with the newness, not from the shiny, now-dried spray of a sauce that reached the page from stove side. I was sure this angle was an easy sell. After all, I clearly remember the first time I ever visited Michael's parents' home. There, clearly, elegantly sitting atop the shiny glass rectangle was the centerpiece of the home, the late, ineffably great

Jean-Louis Palladin's cookbook, *Cooking with the Seasons*. It was in such pristine condition that I dared not touch it. I was there for Passover and I had been rocked by his mother's cooking; her feast a veritable diasporic Thanksgiving! But this book was obviously special; it stood apart from the sullied library that leaned exhausted in the kitchen's pantry.

That's the book I wanted and I was sure Michael did as well. Well, my countless protestations for a book of this kind, a coffee table marvel, sadly, for me and only me I now know, fell on chef's ears. Michael did precisely what he wanted to do. Take a good look at this book, now, now that it's newly minted, fresh in your hands. He wrote the right book. I admit it, he was right. He wrote a book so much more consistent with the essence of what we do in our restaurants, who we are, and why we're in this business in the first place. He wrote a book to help you to throw a party, be it for your kids, for a lover, for your boss and her husband to come over and enjoy, a cookbook in perfect consonance with who he is. He wrote a book that expresses the joy of his world — a world filled with personality, great ingredients, and simple but unusual ideas. Damn him and bless him, this book is a gift to you, to the home chef, to the cook who loves to eat, loves to cook, and loves to provide for those around you. I should be less surprised by this achievement than I am. After nearly two decades of friendship, I should have known better; I wasn't going to get my way and his intuition about what our guests want for food and entertainment is always "right on the money."

So instead of writing a book for himself, or a book to impress other chefs, or a book to promote our restaurants, he wrote a book *for you*. A bountiful gift, a book for you to use, to soil, to dog-ear, to lend, to learn from, to question (oh please, question every page of it), and, in short, to throw a party with. It's not a book about His Royal Chefness, about recipes so brutally labyrinthine that even the experienced cook labors to pull them off in time. It's about the generosity that we try to share every night in Radius, Via Matta, and Great Bay. Allow me to make a claim that few people in America are capable of: Every day when I go to work, I'm happy, no, I'm elated, and I have more fun than anyone is supposed to have. I work with my best friends, they're having just as much fun as I am, and we throw dinner parties every night: three restaurants, three dinner parties, every evening. We can't always go to every one of them, but we inspirit them in our own highly personal and therefore inimitable fashion. Save me, I'm gushing.

A plaque sits over the kitchen door at Radius. Sometimes it's missing, or being cleaned, or graffitied, and as a result it has taken on an apocryphal albeit legendary status. It's our credo, for lack of another word, our promise to ourselves and to our guests. Esti, Michael, and I came up with it together one wine-addled evening, like Matthew, Luke, and John working on the New Testament. (Sorry Michael, sorry Esti, one Christian reference won't kill your parents!) I think it distills all that this book can be for you:

"Please stay tuned as we attempt to improve ourselves as culinarians, one dish at a time; as providers of hospitality, one guest at a time; and as people, one day at a time."

Enjoy this book. Much joy lives in its author and even more can be found in his singular cuisine.

CHEFS ... EGOMANIACS, ALL OF US

It seems like so long ago that I first sat down to create this cookbook, and the truth is I really couldn't decide which direction it should take. At first I thought maybe I should write what I now refer to as the "ego book," a book that was all about me. Me, showing off my exacting knife skills. Me, and the fanciful presentations I had learned over the years. Me, along with recipes that featured a litany of impossible to find, impossible to pronounce, special-order ingredients. A book that would be filled with dishes that, while visually stunning, were probably a bit too complicated for the home cook. Although I am sure it would have been beautiful, I just know it would have ended up on your coffee table, never to see a single splattered sauce stain.

The thought of that book sitting on a coffee table made me reconsider my approach. I realized that this was not the book you wanted, nor was it the one I wanted to write. I wanted to write a book that would inspire and draw you in, full of stories about food, family, history, and how we spend our time together. A book that takes into account today's busy schedules and therefore how very precious the time we get to sit down, break bread, and share a meal really is. Sure it should have gorgeous pictures of food, but only if the recipes can be realistically recreated, the ingredients found and, hey, while we're at it, wouldn't it be great if the recipes actually worked too?

"IT'S ABOUT TIME"

I'd been listening to cooks, both home and professional, for a long time. From these conversations, I realized that I should adopt a unique approach for my book, try to take a fresh and original look at cooking. So instead of my "ego book" here is a book about time — time and its effects on our meals and eating habits. Whether you have a little bit of time or a lot, many of the cooking situations you face in your home will be addressed here. This book is about more than just time measured in seconds, minutes, hours, and days. These ideas on time will rely on rather elastic definitions of the word.

In the last few years, it has become apparent to me that although we have so many modern inventions of convenience, things to make life easier, we as a society have become more and more pressed for time. EZPass for the tolls, DSL for the computers, gas cards for the pump, e-tickets for the plane and on and on the list goes for making our lives easier, faster, and better. But does this all work? From where I'm standing, it seems like we're busier than ever, and one of the areas that seems to be suffering, even with all of these creations, is the way we cook and the way we eat.

Most of us would like to eat well but feel we just don't have enough time. We assume that because we're so busy, then we have to grab something on the fly. This book sets out not only to teach you how to cook and eat well when you're on the go, it also works in reverse for when your soul is crying out for a little bit of culinary therapy. I can't think of a better way to unwind than by spending a couple of hours in the kitchen with a glass of wine, some music on the stereo, and something delicious simmering on the stove.

The chapters in this book are meant to be a guide or source of inspiration for whatever you're in need of today. I know it's impossible to dedicate the same amount of time, every single day, to the meal period. I'm guessing you need some variety, you need some flexibility, and of course you need me to understand that you are busy most (but not all) of the time.

BASEBALL, HOT DOGS, APPLE PIE, AND SOME CAR COMMERCIAL

My love affair with food did not have one of those fairy tale "grew up in the French countryside at his grandmother's apron strings" beginnings; no, nothing quite so dramatic for me. I was born in Brooklyn, New York, to pretty normal, albeit slightly food-obsessed, parents, and I lived for many years in central New Jersey. I was an avid jock in school and really only cared about sports, pretty girls, and getting into trouble. The first job I ever held was as a dishwasher at a local restaurant called the Newsroom. I rode my bicycle to the interview and got hired on the spot, even though I'd never set foot in a restaurant kitchen before. I think what they were really looking for was a young ringer for their Sunday sports teams who could make sure they beat all their rivals, and I fit the bill.

At the Newsroom, I made sure all of the pots, pans, dishes, and glasses were clean, and the owner occasionally allowed me to dabble in the kitchen (if dabbling means making late-night burgers for the last-call drunks). I went on to perform just about every job at that restaurant: busboy, host, server, prep-cook, and although I never imagined that food and cooking would become so important to me, the Newsroom is definitely where I caught the restaurant bug. Working at that restaurant was not just a way to make a little spending money, I actually enjoyed being there, being part of all the social activity. Everyone was having a great time and I loved being in the middle of it, even if I was just the dishwasher. As I got older, I became more and more transfixed with all things associated with cooking. I was smitten with the interaction between restaurant and guest, and after several misguided career moves that I will chalk up to youthful exuberance, I eventually enrolled in culinary school and soon realized that cooking professionally was what I was meant to do with my life. I was driven like never before, and my goal was to put myself on a path to success. After graduation, I sought out the best possible on-the-job education by working for the greatest chefs and restaurateurs who would let me in the door. It did not take me long to realize that graduating from chef's school doesn't make you a chef; in fact, it was many years before I would wear that title with great pride and responsibility.

I guess it's fair to say that when it comes to preparing food, I might think a bit differently from most home cooks. But I wrote this book with the home cook completely in mind. Many people think that I have some special tricks up my sleeve when it comes to cooking, but I don't. When they absolutely persist in knowing what the secret to my success is, I lean in and whisper "salt and pepper." What I have attempted to do with these recipes is to show you how easy great food can be. Good cooking starts with good ingredients. Cooking is all about buying the best ingredients (humble or luxurious), then going into the meal with a game plan and enjoying the process of creating something from start to finish. Trust me on the planning ahead part — just because you're cooking doesn't mean you can't enjoy the party. The chapter in this book on throwing the ultimate barbeque exemplifies this approach. Good barbeques are about smart thinking, great ingredients, and planning ahead.

A-N-T-H-O-N-Y!!!!!

When I was a kid, it seemed all of my friends and I had to leave the playground around the same time — always when the streetlights came on. This was the time that everyone in the neighborhood went home to eat dinner with their families, and things at my house were no different. Being together around the dinner table as a family was the most important time of the day for us.

Now, with so many homes that have two working parents and everyone being so busy, it seems the type of family meal that I grew up with has become practically nonexistent. I set aside a complete chapter in this book on how incredibly significant the time spent at the dinner table can be, hoping that maybe a few nostalgic stories and some great recipes will get people to rekindle this very important daily ritual.

Since we're all probably guilty of not taking great care of ourselves when we're feeling frazzled by our busy schedules — times when we need pampering the most — I've also included in one chapter great food that can be made in thirty minutes or less, satisfying meals for when time is really of the essence and going to the drive-thru just isn't on your dance card.

"DHAAAAARRRLING, THIS IS DELICIOUS; YOU MUST GIVE ME THE RECIPE"

At one time or another we've all felt unsure of ourselves in the kitchen, as though the task at hand is beyond our abilities, but the situation — a first date, future in-laws dropping by, the boss coming for dinner — calls for us to "shine." I have included recipes for just such an occasion. The idea is to give you some tools and tricks so that when you make these recipes, you'll look as if you've been moonlighting in one of America's best kitchens instead of going to that Monday night bowling league. Same idea with times of celebration; everyone wonders how to make these occasions special without being obvious. I've given you a road map for some really great ways to celebrate at home, and hopefully you'll not only enjoy eating the meal, you'll love making it as well.

As you get further into this book, you'll see that in addition to being about time, it's also about paying proper respect. Respect for the power and importance of well-prepared food, quality time spent together, and tradition. I couldn't possibly pass up the chance to comment on the subject of paying respect to true, authentic Italian cooking, which is not the bastardized, watered down version we get all too often in American restaurants. So I've devoted a chapter to the classic, unadulterated dishes on the menu at Via Matta, the Italian restaurant I own with my business partners, Christopher Myers and Esti Parsons. Likewise, another chapter features the greatest hits from our Modern French restaurant, Radius. Equal respect (at the same time) for both the Italians and the French — now that's a first!

JAMES JOYCE, WILLIAM SHAKESPEARE, OR PATRICIA WELLS? I'LL TAKE PATRICIA WELLS

I love cookbooks. I read the best ones the way others might read classic novels. I enjoy finding out what makes different authors tick, what has motivated them to share certain recipes, and how they came to tell their particular stories. *It's About Time* was written while sitting at my kitchen table, mostly late at night, with a tape measure, assorted spoons, and a timer next to the computer. I wanted to get every detail right so that these recipes would inspire you and give you the confidence to make great food any and every time.

Writing a cookbook is a long and sometimes tedious process and at times I struggled to articulate convictions I felt deeply but had never put into words. I think I was surprised to find it such an intimate and introspective experience. It certainly has been rewarding for me, and I hope all of the late nights pay off for both of us, and this book becomes a permanent fixture in your kitchen. (By the way, it makes a lovely gift. . . .)

Finally, I want to thank you for reading my book. If you've gotten to this point in the introduction (and not just flipped through all of the pretty pictures), then you and I have something in common: we want the whole story, every bit of it. I've written this book for you, the fearless and somewhat curious home cook.

It's my hope that you'll open this cookbook over and over again, and nothing would please me more than to see it end up dog-eared and splattered with sauce stains.

Michael Schlow
September, 2004

READ THIS FIRST!

SEASONING, SALT, AND THE COMMON-SENSE DICE

Lots of cookbooks say things like "salt and pepper to taste"; I've complicated matters further in this book by sometimes adding "sugar to taste." What in the world does this mean to you, the home cook?

The sensation that comes from tasting food is unique from person to person. What seems salty to one is bland to another. "Here, taste this, I think it's too spicy," might elicit "Wimp!" from someone who has an asbestos palette. When I write "to taste," I am leaving this part up to you and your personal preferences.

It is my opinion that pretty much all foods need something to lift them to a higher level. My 93-year-old grandfather, Sol, would disagree. When I have had the pleasure of cooking for him, it is guaranteed that he will start to question what it is that I am preparing for the meal. When I tell him my intentions, he usually responds with "No monkey business. I want nice, clean food." My grandmother, Ruth, will then chime in with "You know, Michael, I don't cook with any salt." Yes Grandma, we know, we know.

I think that you need to approach cooking and seasoning with simple common sense. Our palettes can only decipher five tastes—salty, sweet, spicy, bitter, and tart. If an ingredient is inherently salty (like anchovies, black olives, capers), then the dish probably won't require as much salt. Dishes that contain things like potatoes, mushrooms, pasta, or polenta will require more aggressive seasoning because, for some reason, these products just crave more salt to bring out their natural goodness. Same thing goes for pepper and sugar. Hot chiles in the dish? Then go easy on the pepper. If there is a high amount of acid in a dish, then you might need a little pinch of sugar to balance out the tartness.

There must be some scientific data to back up my claims; why things like starches are in need of more aggressive seasoning than say, clams, which have a natural brininess that makes you think twice before adding another pinch of salt, but for now let's just leave it up to how things taste to you and your taste buds.

I always use kosher salt. I never use iodized table salt, never. Although there are many people on low-sodium diets, there is a new, different kind of salt craze going on in the world when menus list dishes like Carpaccio of Yellowtail with Pink Lava Salt from the Northside of the Great Barrier Reef. I still find kosher salt to be the best thing to use in a restaurant kitchen, and it's what I have sitting next to the stove at my house. Since we usually use pinches of salt, with our fingers and not a spoon, I also find it the easiest to use. All salts have different levels of saltiness; just because it says "kosher salt" on the box doesn't mean that different brands are the same. Try it youself: taste the difference between Diamond Crystal and Morton's kosher salt; there is a distinct difference in the size of the flake and the level of saltiness, so use what you like best.

. . .

Another item worth mentioning is the art of dicing. In this book you will see directions like "small dice," "finely diced," "medium dice," "sliced thinly," and so on. When I was in culinary school, the chefs would actually take out a tape measure and inspect all sides, tops, and bottoms to make sure that you were indeed making a true *brunoise* of carrot. Anything that did not meet code was tossed into the stockpot, usually with a grunt and a snort that quickly made you realize that you had not met the task at hand. No need for that sort of behavior here. Rather than get really specific and technical in this book about whether small dice is $1/8$ or $1/16$ inch, let's keep the tape measure in the kitchen's junk drawer, and go, yet again, with common sense. When cutting vegetables, herbs, fish, or meat, take a look at the other ingredients in the recipe and make sure that everything is roughly the same size, yet still gives you some variety in texture and shape. For example, if you are making a dish with tiny French green lentils and the recipe calls for bacon, you want to cut the bacon into small squares, similar in size to the lentils, rather than big, overpowering slabs, so the bacon has a "relationship," something in common, with the lentils.

Another example can be seen in the recipe Gnocchi with Vegetable Pearls (page 145). If the gnocchi are rolled small, then the pearls should also be small. Make the gnocchi larger, increase the size of the pearls.

All ingredients in a recipe should have a symbiotic relationship with one another. Whether it be flavor profile, size, shape, texture, they have to work together to create something delicious and memorable.

Seasoning and good knife skills are two of the most important aspects of cooking. When seasoning, don't try to "nail" it with the first try. Rather, go about it in small steps (hence the "to taste"), adding a little bit at a time. You can always add more at the end, but it is really hard to balance a recipe once it has been over-seasoned. And with the cutting, don't worry too much if it isn't perfectly square or round, just don't give up on your dream of someday being able to make perfect *brunoise* of carrots, which, by the way, are $1/16$ x $1/16$ x $1/16$ inch. . . . Careful — don't cut yourself!

Chapter 1

TIME TO EAT AND NOW

DISHES THAT CAN BE ON THE TABLE
IN 30 MINUTES OR LESS

Doesn't it seem like you're in a hurry more often these days? Schedules have become so hectic and crowded; dinners are planned weeks or months in advance with friends and even family. Life is so full and stress levels so high that perhaps you're wondering if you have time to read this. Maybe you've even forgotten to eat, so now your blood sugar is starting to drop. Just the idea of cooking implies something that might take a long time; you're hungry and you want to eat now!

When you're this busy, certain dining decisions reflect perceived ease. Maybe you'll go to a restaurant or the drive-thru. If you've decided on cooking, you might go to the pantry and gaze at the cans for a while, maybe end up looking in the freezer for some long-lost who-knows-what, and then turn to the microwave. (For the record, putting something in the microwave does not constitute "cooking" in my book.)

Trust me, perceived ease in the kitchen is almost always an illusion. There is nothing enjoyable or satisfying about opening cans, thawing frozen foods, or pressing microwave buttons, and the food is never half as good. I'm frequently tempted myself, but I try to be strong. When I go to the supermarket, I don't fill my cart up with canned and frozen products. Why would I buy canned asparagus? I'm still going to have to heat it up, I still have to use fire. Why not blanch fresh asparagus, which will taste so much better?

In this chapter I'm going to make this as easy as I can for you. I'm going to show you that cooking good food does not have to take a long time. I'm going to assume that if you're pressed for time in cooking, you're going to be pressed for time in cleaning as well — so some of the recipes in this chapter require only one pot or pan. Who has time to clean? We've got soccer practice to go to!

And if you don't have time to cook or clean, shopping is probably a big deal too. You've got to be able to get these ingredients at any supermarket, where your time-saving strategies should begin. Think thin pork chops, because they cook about five times faster than those big double-cut ones. Buy the baby spinach that comes already cleaned in an air-tight bag and that will last a week or more in your refrigerator.

Making dinner does not have to be a time-consuming chore. It can be fast and easy with terrific results. Try putting everything aside: sit, breathe, and eat.
It's ironic but true — when you think you can relax the least is usually when you need to the most.

WARM SHRIMP SALAD
WITH WHITE BEANS AND ARUGULA

When I worked at Sapore di Mare in the Hamptons, the menu featured a simple salad of perfectly cooked white beans, lemon, and a few slivers of fresh red onion served on a bed of arugula and drizzled with fruity extra-virgin olive oil. This jazzed-up version adds shrimp and tomatoes to the basic salad, and people ask for the recipe whenever I serve it. This recipe yields appetizer portions, but you can double it to create a more substantial entrée, ideal for an early autumn lunch served al fresco. Accompany with plenty of bread to soak up the flavorful broth.

TRUC It is not necessary to rinse shrimp after shelling and deveining them — the water washes away a lot of flavor. To peel and devein: Use a paring knife to cut along the black line on the outside curl. Peel the shell away from the body and use the tip of your knife to clear away the intestinal vein.

NOTE To cook dried beans: Soak 1 pound dried beans overnight in plenty of water. Drain them, transfer to a heavy pot, and cover by a couple inches with water. Add 2 tablespoons salt and 1 cup of olive oil, and bring to a simmer over medium heat. Reduce heat to low, and cook gently until tender. Timing varies according to the freshness and type of bean, but plan on about an hour. You will only need 1 cup cooked beans for this salad. Serve leftovers as a side dish, or use in soups or in Rigatoni with Soppressata, White Beans, Tomato, and Black Olives (page 64).

ANOTHER NOTE If fresh cranberry beans are in season, use them instead of cannellini beans.

Makes 4 first courses

- Heat olive oil and garlic in a medium sauce pot over high heat and cook until the garlic begins to turn golden brown.
- Add the onion and cook for 1 minute.
- Add the rosemary.
- Add salt, pepper, and crushed red pepper flakes to taste.
- Add the shrimp and cook for 1 to 2 minutes, until the shrimp just start to turn color but are not completely cooked.
- Add the beans, tomatoes, and the vegetable stock and simmer 2 minutes. (If you are using the canned beans, add only the stock and the tomatoes.)
- Add the canned beans now, if you are using them.
- Add the arugula and simmer 30 seconds to 1 minute, until slightly wilted.
- Squeeze the lemon into the warm salad and taste for seasoning.
- Let salad cool slightly, then divide between four small bowls and serve while still warm.

2 ounces (¼ cup) extra-virgin olive oil

½ clove garlic, very thinly sliced

½ red onion, thinly sliced

1 pinch fresh rosemary, chopped

Salt, pepper, and crushed red pepper flakes

16 large shrimp, shelled and deveined

1 cup cooked white beans, preferably cannellini (canned may be substituted)

2 plum tomatoes, cut into medium dice

4 ounces (½ cup) Clear Vegetable Stock (page 214; chicken stock can be substituted)

2 loosely packed cups arugula (2 large handfuls), cleaned

Juice of 1 lemon

STEAMED PRINCE EDWARD ISLAND MUSSELS

WITH SPICY TOMATO AND HERB BROTH

2 ounces (¼ cup) extra-virgin olive oil

½ clove garlic, thinly sliced

1 shallot, minced

Salt, pepper, and crushed red pepper flakes

1 large pinch fresh thyme leaves, chopped

2 plum tomatoes, finely diced (save everything, juice and all)

Juice of 1 lemon

2 ounces (¼ cup) water

40 to 45 P.E.I. mussels, rinsed of any grit and debearded, if needed

2 tablespoons butter

2 teaspoons finely chopped fresh chives

I could eat a giant bowl of this for dinner just about any time of the year. Serve this with lots of grilled French bread, a light salad, and a glass or three of really good white wine and you have yourself a fantastic, effortless dinner. I suggest buying the Prince Edward Island (P.E.I.) cultivated mussels. Why? Unlike wild mussels, which live on the ocean floor, cultivated mussels are grown on ropes (yes, ropes!) suspended in the bays and inlets of Prince Edward Island, so they are not full of sand, and they don't require the painstaking scrubbing normally associated with preparing mussels. *Painstaking* and *scrubbing* are two words I try not to associate with my cooking — scrubbing is for cleaning, and anything painstaking I would just as soon avoid.

NOTE Choose a large sauce pot for this recipe. To allow room for the shells to open, the mussels should not come more than halfway up the sides of the pot.

Makes 2 generous servings

- Preheat the oven to 250°F.
- Place the olive oil and garlic in a large sauce pot and cook over high heat until the garlic is light golden brown.
- Add the shallot and cook 1 minute.
- Add a pinch each of salt, pepper, and crushed red pepper flakes.
- Add the thyme.
- Add the tomatoes, lemon juice, and water, and cook for 1 to 2 minutes.
- Add the mussels and cover the pot.
- The mussels are cooked once they open completely. Do not continue cooking past this point, or they will shrivel and become tough.
- Divide the mussels evenly between two large ovenproof bowls, leaving all of the broth in the pot. Place the bowls in the oven to keep warm while you finish the sauce.
- Remove the sauce pot from the heat and whisk the butter into the broth. (An immersion blender, known formally as a handheld electric burr mixer, is great for this.)
- Add the chives, taste the sauce, and adjust the seasoning if needed.
- Remove the bowls from the oven and spoon the sauce over the mussels.
- Serve with grilled bread (see truc, page 60) for dipping.

SHAVED ZUCCHINI AND MUSHROOM SALAD

WITH ARUGULA, PARMIGIANO-REGGIANO, AND LEMON

This is one of the most popular salads I serve at our Italian restaurant, Via Matta. It comes together in no time because nothing is actually cooked, a real plus in a busy restaurant kitchen where you sometimes have to deal with impatient, hungry guests who are demanding to know where their food is. The paper-thin vegetables have a wonderful texture, and the ingredients combine to create a dish that is both satisfying and refreshing. If there happens to be a mandoline lying around the house, break it out to slice the vegetables for this salad.

Makes 2 large salads

- Combine the zucchini, mushrooms, onion, and capers in a small bowl.
- Add the juice of half a lemon.
- Add 2 ounces (4 tablespoons) olive oil.
- Season with salt and pepper, and toss to coat evenly.
- In a separate bowl, drizzle juice from the remaining lemon half and 1 ounce (2 tablespoons) olive oil over the arugula. Toss to combine.
- Season with salt and pepper to taste.
- Divide the arugula between two dinner plates.
- Place the raw vegetable salad on top of the arugula.
- Garnish the salad with the shaved Parmigiano-Reggiano.
- Drizzle more olive oil over the salad, if you wish, and serve.

1 medium zucchini, cut in half lengthwise, then sliced crosswise as thinly as possible

5 large button mushrooms, halved, then sliced as thinly as possible

½ red onion, thinly sliced

12 to 18 capers

1 lemon, halved

3 ounces (6 tablespoons) extra-virgin olive oil, plus additional for drizzling over finished salad

Salt and pepper

1 large bunch arugula, rinsed and spun dry

6 very thin (shaved) slices good-quality Parmigiano-Reggiano cheese

ENDIVE AND RADICCHIO SALAD

WITH BLUE CHEESE, WALNUTS, AND GOLDEN RAISINS

½ teaspoon Dijon mustard

1 pinch fresh rosemary, chopped

3 ounces (6 tablespoons) extra-virgin olive oil

1 ounce (2 tablespoons) sherry vinegar (balsamic can be substituted)

Salt and pepper, to taste

3 heads radicchio, broken into leaves and torn into bite-sized pieces

3 heads endive, cut crosswise into thin slices

½ red onion, thinly sliced

½ cup walnut pieces

3 tablespoons blue cheese, crumbled into small pieces (you can choose the quality and brand)

3 tablespoons golden raisins

Italian parsley for garnish (optional)

Some of the ingredients in this salad are excellent "on-hand" items for those in a hurry; the blue cheese, walnuts, and raisins will keep for a very long time, and they are a distinctive addition to many dishes. Some diced grilled chicken will make this salad even more substantial, and diced smoked bacon sends it over the top! I cannot count the number of times I've made a meal out of this salad when I'm home cooking for just myself.

NOTE Any extra dressing will keep in the refrigerator for a week. Use it to dress mixed greens or to drizzle on grilled fish.

Makes 2 salads, big enough for lunch

- Whisk together the mustard, rosemary, olive oil, vinegar, salt, and pepper in a small bowl.
- Place all the remaining ingredients except the parsley in a large salad bowl.
- Pour the vinaigrette over the salad, mix well, adjust the seasoning, and garnish with whole parsley leaves, if desired.

BABY SPINACH SALAD

WITH SMOKED BACON, RED ONION, AND GOAT CHEESE

3 strips thick-sliced smoked bacon, each strip cut into 6 square pieces

2 loosely packed cups baby spinach (2 large handfuls), cleaned

¼ large red onion, thinly sliced

2 ounces (¼ cup) extra-virgin olive oil

1 ounce (2 tablespoons) balsamic vinegar

1 pinch fresh thyme leaves

4 tablespoons crumbled goat cheese

Salt and pepper

When I'm in a rush or in need of something quick, easy, and delicious, I often make this salad. If you can find it, buy the baby spinach that comes already cleaned in a vacuum-sealed pouch. You won't have to spend any time washing the dirt from the spinach, and you'll be that much closer to the finished dish!

TRUC To slice an onion, cut off both the top and bottom ends, peel it, then cut it in half lengthwise. Place each half cut-side down with the root end toward you, then slice lengthwise, working from right to left (or left to right, if you are left-handed). The onion will come apart easily into uniform, eye-appealing crescents.

NOTE Don't throw that bacon fat away! It can be reserved in a clean coffee can — perhaps forever — in the refrigerator. The fat imparts a fantastic, slightly smoky flavor to foods, just the thing for frying your Sunday morning hash browns or basting chicken or pork as it roasts in the oven. If you really want to go for broke, replace the butter with a little bacon fat when making your next grilled cheese sandwich.

Serves 2 as a first course; double the recipe to serve as an entrée

- Cook the bacon slowly over low heat in a medium sauté pan until slightly crisp.
- Pour off the excess fat, saving 2 ounces (¼ cup) for the dressing, and remove the pan from the heat.
- Place the spinach and onion in a large mixing bowl.
- Add the oil, vinegar, and thyme to the bacon and bacon fat.
- Add salt and pepper to the bacon mixture. Taste, and adjust seasoning.
- Pour the warm bacon vinaigrette over the spinach mixture.
- Add the goat cheese and toss gently (with tongs — it's going to be hot!).
- Test seasoning again, adjust with salt and pepper if needed, and serve on two large plates.

PENNE
WITH ITALIAN SAUSAGE AND TOMATO

Once the water is boiling, you can have this on the table in 20 minutes or less. I often make this penne for my brother when I visit him, because it reminds us of the summers we spent working in the Hamptons together. I would whip this up, and then we would go out after work to see what kind of trouble we could find. Usually the pasta was the highlight of the night; but not always. . . .

NOTE Always cook pasta in lightly salted boiling water. If the water is not at a full boil, the pasta will turn out gummy, and pasta has better flavor if it absorbs salt as it cooks. On a related note, never add oil to the cooking water. Oil only coats the pasta and prevents the sauce from adhering to it.

ANOTHER NOTE Don't be tentative when seasoning sauces for pasta. Remember, you have to add enough salt, pepper, and red pepper flakes not only for the sauce but to create a balance of flavors once the pasta has been added. So season the sauce accordingly, and there will be no need for additional tinkering after it has been combined with the pasta.

Makes 2 generous bowls of pasta, plenty for a main course

8 ounces penne rigate

3 sweet Italian sausages, removed from their skins and crumbled

½ clove garlic, sliced

Salt, pepper, and crushed red pepper flakes

1 large pinch fresh rosemary, chopped

3 ripe plum tomatoes, cut into medium dice

1 tablespoon butter

½ cup grated Parmigiano-Reggiano cheese

15 to 20 whole Italian parsley leaves

- Bring plenty of water to a boil in a large pot. When the water is about to boil, add a few pinches salt.
- Meanwhile, brown sausage in a medium sauce pot over medium-low heat.
- No oil or butter is needed yet. Move the sausage around with a wooden spoon as it starts to brown.
- After 3 to 5 minutes, when the sausage is almost cooked through, add the garlic and cook for 2 more minutes.
- Pour off all but about 3 ounces (6 tablespoons) of the fat.
- When the water comes to a boil, drop in the pasta, stir briefly to keep from sticking, and cook until al dente, 7 to 9 minutes, depending on the pasta.
- Add three large pinches of salt, two pinches of pepper, one pinch of crushed red pepper flakes, and the rosemary to the sausage mixture.
- Add the tomatoes, turn the heat to high, and continue to cook until most of the liquid in the sauce has evaporated, 5 to 7 minutes. Stir often to prevent sticking.
- Check the pasta for doneness.
- Adjust the seasonings in the sauce, if needed.
- Stir the butter into the sauce.
- When the pasta is done, strain, add it to the sauce, and cook over high heat for 2 minutes, stirring to combine.
- Add the cheese and parsley and stir for 30 seconds to incorporate. The pasta won't be drowning in an ocean of sauce; rather, there will be just enough to coat it lightly.
- Serve in two large bowls.

QUICK PORK CHOPS

WITH HOT CHERRY PEPPERS, SEARED CAULIFLOWER, AND ONIONS

Most people don't think of pork chops as a quick supper, but thin-cut chops take very little time to cook. If you happen to dread cauliflower, just give this recipe a chance; I promise it will change your mind. The cauliflower comes out slightly crunchy and spicy, and the sautéing gives it a light caramelization that sweetens its flavor. Sometimes I skip the pork chops altogether and make a meal out of just the cauliflower. It really is that good.

Makes a quick dinner for 2

- Preheat the oven to 350°F.
- Heat the extra-virgin olive oil in a large sauté pan over high heat for 1 minute.
- Add the cauliflower florets.
- Cook without moving or seasoning for 1 to 2 minutes, until the cauliflower begins to turn golden brown.
- While the cauliflower is cooking, place a very large, ovenproof sauté pan over high heat, add the canola oil, and heat for 30 seconds. (You can use two pans to avoid crowding.)
- Season the pork chops with salt and pepper, put them in the pan with the canola oil, and sauté gently, 1 minute per side.
- Place the chops in the oven and roast for 9 to 12 minutes, depending on their thickness, turning once every 3 minutes to promote even cooking.
- When the pork chops are done, remove them from the oven and let them rest 2 to 3 minutes in the pan.
- While the pork chops are in the oven, let the cauliflower continue cooking until almost tender, stirring to brown all sides, about 4 minutes. Remove from heat to prevent overcooking, if needed.
- When the cauliflower starts to become tender (but still has a bit of crunch), add the red onion and cook for 2 more minutes.
- Add the hot peppers, bread crumbs, butter, salt, and pepper and cook until the cauliflower is tender, about 2 minutes. Remove from heat.
- Add the cheese and parsley to the cauliflower mixture, and toss. Return to the burner and cook for 1 minute over medium heat.
- Place two pork chops on each plate and smother with the cauliflower mixture.
- Squeeze the lemon over the top, and start eating!

2 ounces (4 tablespoons) extra-virgin olive oil

½ head cauliflower, cut into small florets

2 ounces (4 tablespoons) canola oil

4 thin pork chops (loin, no more than ¾-inch thick)

Salt and pepper

½ red onion, thinly sliced

2 tablespoons sliced hot cherry peppers (fresh or canned)

3 tablespoons seasoned bread crumbs (store-bought are fine)

1 tablespoon butter

3 tablespoons grated Parmigiano-Reggiano cheese

3 tablespoons coarsely chopped Italian parsley

Juice of 1 lemon

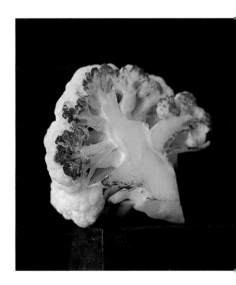

GRILLED SWORDFISH
WITH CORN, TOMATO, AND LIME

FOR THE
SALSA

2 ounces (¼ cup) extra-
virgin olive oil

½ red onion, thinly sliced

4 ears corn, husked and
cleaned, kernels removed
from the cobs

3 ripe plum tomatoes,
cut into medium dice

1 tablespoon chopped
fresh cilantro

1 pinch cayenne pepper

Salt and pepper

Juice of 1 lime

FOR THE
SWORDFISH

4 7-ounce swordfish
fillets, cut 1½ inches
thick (Don't be shy—
ask the guy at the fish
counter to portion and
clean the fish for you.)

Salt and pepper

1 pinch cayenne pepper

½ tablespoon chopped
fresh cilantro

2 ounces (¼ cup) extra-
virgin olive oil

Juice of 1 lime

Fresh cilantro sprigs,
for garnish (optional)

If you have one of those high-tech barbecue grills with a burner on the side, you can make the salsa at the same time you grill the fish. Otherwise, prepare the salsa indoors on the stovetop while the grill is heating, and keep it in a warm spot while the swordfish cooks. You can also serve it at room temperature or even slightly chilled.

TRUC To remove corn kernels from the cob: Pull the husks from each ear of corn and rub off all the strands of silk. Hold the corn at an angle over a baking dish and run a sharp knife from the top of the cob to the bottom, cutting away the kernels but leaving the cob.

Makes dinner for 4

FOR THE SALSA
- Heat the olive oil in a large sauté pan over high heat.
- Add the onion and sauté for 2 minutes.
- Add the corn, lower the heat to medium-high, and sauté for 2 minutes.
- Add the tomatoes and sauté for 2 minutes.
- Stir in the cilantro, a pinch of cayenne pepper, salt and pepper, and the lime juice.
- Taste and adjust seasoning, if needed.
- Keep warm while grilling the swordfish.

FOR THE SWORDFISH
- Turn the grill to high.
- Season the swordfish with salt, pepper, and a pinch of cayenne pepper, then rub the cilantro onto both sides of each fillet.
- Lightly brush both sides of the swordfish with the olive oil.
- When the grill is hot, put the swordfish on, reduce the heat to medium-high, and cook for 2 minutes.
- Rotate each piece a quarter of a turn with your tongs — from 3 o'clock to 6 o'clock in other words — without turning it over. This will "mark" the fish, giving it a professional-looking grill mark on the side that is face-down.
- Cook for 3 more minutes.
- Flip the fish over and grill 3 minutes.
- Give the swordfish a quarter turn to mark the other side.
- Cook for another 2 to 3 minutes, or until the fish is just cooked through. It will be slightly firm, but still juicy.
- Remove the swordfish from the grill and drizzle with the lime juice.

TO SERVE
- Place a large spoonful of the corn salsa in the center of four dinner plates.
- Arrange the swordfish on top of the corn mixture, garnish with cilantro sprigs, and serve.

CHICKEN BREAST
WITH SPICY ZUCCHINI AND SNAP PEAS

2 large boneless chicken breasts, skin removed

2 ounces (4 tablespoons) extra-virgin olive oil

Salt and pepper

1 cup snap peas, trimmed

3 ounces (6 tablespoons) water

½ red onion, thinly sliced

½ medium zucchini, quartered lengthwise, then sliced crosswise into ¼-inch thick quarter-circles

1 ripe plum tomato, cut into small dice

⅛ teaspoon togarashi (cayenne pepper can be substituted)

Juice of half a lemon

This dish incorporates a little cooking maneuver I use at home to save time. Basically, I cheat: I throw the snap peas right in the pan after the chicken has been browned. In my restaurants, we would blanch the peas in salted, boiling water, then "shock" them in ice water as part of the advance preparation. For the sake of time, it's harmless enough to skip that step, although I'd rather my cooks didn't find out; they might not be sympathetic to our need for speed.

NOTE I love the flavor of a condiment called *togarashi*. I first discovered it in a Japanese restaurant, where it added a spicy, interesting note to a soup called *yosenabe*. Togarashi is made from Thai chiles, orange zest, white and black sesame seeds, fennel seeds, and hemp (yes, hemp, and no, nobody ever got stoned from using togarashi on their food). You can find it in Asian markets, where it often goes by the name *schichimi togarashi*.

Makes 2 really quick dinners

- Preheat the oven to 300°F.
- Pound the chicken breasts a few times with a meat mallet to flatten slightly.
- Heat 1 ounce (2 tablespoons) olive oil over medium-high heat in a nonstick sauté pan.
- Season the chicken breasts with salt and pepper.
- Add the chicken to the pan and gently brown on both sides, about 2 minutes per side.
- Transfer the chicken breasts to a baking sheet and let finish cooking in the oven, 7 to 9 minutes, or until cooked through but still juicy.
- Meanwhile, place the snap peas and water in the sauté pan. Cover the pan and cook for 2 minutes. Remove the lid and continue to cook until most of the water has evaporated.
- Add the remaining 1 ounce (2 tablespoons) olive oil and the onion to the snap peas, and sauté for 2 minutes.
- Add the zucchini and sauté for 1 to 2 minutes, until almost tender.
- Add the tomato, the togarashi (or cayenne pepper), salt, and pepper, and cook 1 more minute.
- Taste the vegetables and adjust the seasoning, if needed.
- Check the chicken breasts for doneness. (I do what you do, by the way: take my piece and slice into it on the sly to see how we're doing.)
- When finished cooking, place each chicken breast in the center of a plate, top with the vegetables, squeeze the lemon juice over all, and serve.

FRESH STRAWBERRIES
WITH BALSAMIC VINEGAR AND BASIL

Quite possibly the quickest dessert I know. When I first heard about strawberries being served with balsamic vinegar and basil, it sounded like a mad scientist's experiment gone awry. But this is actually a classic Northern Italian dessert, and the interplay of flavors is surprisingly harmonious.

Quick dessert for 4

- Slice the strawberries in halves or quarters, depending on their size.
- Place all of the ingredients in a mixing bowl.
- Let macerate in the refrigerator for 10 to 30 minutes, as time allows.
- Serve in individual serving bowls, with cookies, whipped cream, ice cream, pound cake. . . .

4 cups strawberries, washed and hulled

½ cup sugar

4 ounces (½ cup) balsamic vinegar

1 tablespoon honey

12 basil leaves, torn into small pieces

A few turns of the pepper mill

Chapter 2

TIME TO GET THE FAMILY TOGETHER

ELBOWS OFF THE TABLE

When I was growing up, my family ate dinner together just about every night. There were no excuses — you had better be there, and you had better be on time. When the streetlights came on, you knew it was time to go home. Even my father, who was a lawyer in the town we lived in, would come home for a few hours. He would eat dinner with us, talk to us, and then go back to work after we went upstairs, allegedly to do our homework. Unless there was a special occasion, this was the way it was done.

Unfortunately, I think this type of routine has been lost in many families. Now sitting down and eating dinner together is seen as a special occasion. Back then, whether we were aware of it or not, the dinner table was where it was at. I can look back on those days and say that many a life's lesson was taught in my parents' kitchen. Our behavior and manners; learning to argue a point, religion, or politics; the meaning of real patience, all stemmed from our time together at the dinner table. Maybe there is no way to recover this ritual completely. Everyone is so busy and has so much to do, with both parents working, Little League, violin lessons, PTA meetings and so on. But I do think it's worth making a concerted effort to bring back the family dinner, at least once a week.

Now here's the tricky part. It's going to be the same dinner for everyone. I know what you're thinking: "But everyone in my family likes different things." I've been to houses like yours — in fact, my sister is currently running her own private family restaurant where she feeds three customers a night: her sons. With the invention of the microwave and the ease of frozen individual dinners it's: "Noah, what do you want for dinner? How about you Joshua, what do feel like having tonight? And you, Zachary, what do you want to eat?"

There were no choices regarding dinner when we were growing up!

I grew up in a household where food was important, I mean really important, and not for its basic nutritional sustenance. I'm talking about food freaks here. A family completely consumed with the experience of eating and dining. Food, food, food, food . . . the sensation that came with eating! We would be eating breakfast and the conversation would be about what we were going to have for dinner. What kinds of exotic dishes would we try next? Were we going to try the new Indian restaurant around the corner? Could we order an appetizer?

Most of this behavior was due to my mother; I can safely say she was the culprit behind this food thing. I know for a fact I was the only kid on the block whose mother had homemade *garam masala* in the cupboard in 1978. Back when most people thought Chinese food meant pu-pu platters, lo mein, and egg rolls, she was making hot-and-sour soup from scratch. She even had fresh mozzarella in the fridge just waiting for the tomatoes and basil from her garden.

She had the audacity (when we were not paying attention) to switch our iceberg lettuce and our favorite bottled dressing with this spicy green leafy thing called *arugula* that she tossed with balsamic vinegar and extra-virgin olive oil. Back then she tried to get it past us by telling us, "Kids, we're having salad from the garden tonight!"

I certainly would not be where I am today without my parents. I know everybody says that, but I truly mean it. I trace a lot of it back to those dinners together and being around the table with my family; listening to my parents talk, and the questions that would naturally arise. No telephone calls were allowed during dinner, and certainly no TV; often we didn't get up from the table even when we were done eating. We'd just sit there for a little while longer, actually talking to each other. It's my hope that you will pass on similar experiences to your family. The family dinner really is such an important moment in our everyday lives, it would be tragic if it became just a special occasion.

RED WINE–BRAISED BRISKET

WITH MUSHROOMS, TOMATO, AND ROSEMARY

This brisket is good home cooking at its finest. It is one of those ultimate comfort foods — everyone around the table will feel safe and secure when they taste this.

All is good in the world tonight.

The recipe can be prepared several days ahead, and the brisket freezes beautifully. It's nice to have things like this tucked away for those days when you really don't feel like cooking. Serve it with just about anything: potato puree, buttered noodles, more vegetables.

TRUC When slicing meats, always try to cut across the grain of the meat, and remember to let the meat rest a few minutes (or more) before you slice into it. Why? As meats finish roasting, their juices are rolling around like boiling water in a pot. After the meat rests briefly, the juices cool and settle into place, attached to the strands of protein in the meat. If you let meats rest after cooking, the juices won't leak out onto the counter when the meat is sliced. They will stay put, making the meat more flavorful, juicy, and tender.

NOTE Choose a pan with high sides for this recipe. It must be deep enough to hold the brisket, the vegetables, and the sauce. You also have to remember where you stashed the lid to the pan, or you can cover the pan tightly with aluminum foil.

Serves 6

- Preheat the oven to 300°F.
- Put the olive oil in a roasting pan or a large, ovenproof sauté pan and place over high heat.
- Season the brisket generously with salt and pepper.
- When the oil is hot, gently sear the meat on all sides until good and golden brown.
- Remove meat from the pan and set aside on a serving platter.
- Add the garlic, onion, carrot, and celery to the pan and cook for 2 minutes, still on high heat.
- Add the rosemary and a bit more salt and pepper.
- Add the butter and cook until melted.
- Lower the heat to medium and sprinkle in the flour. Cook for 2 minutes, stirring constantly.
- Add the red wine, raise the heat to high, and cook for 2 minutes, scraping the bottom of the pan so the ingredients do not stick.
- Add the tomatoes, crushing them a bit with your hands — yes, your hands — as you put them into the pan.
- Add the chicken stock and the quartered button mushrooms, and stir everything around in the pan.

directions are continued on following page

Ingredients

- 3 ounces (6 tablespoons) extra-virgin olive oil
- 1 large brisket (3 to 4 pounds), trimmed of any excess fat
- Salt and pepper
- ½ clove garlic, thinly sliced
- 1 onion, cut into medium dice
- 1 large carrot, peeled, halved lengthwise, and then sliced ¼-inch thick
- 1 stalk celery, sliced ¼-inch thick
- 1 teaspoon chopped fresh rosemary
- 3 tablespoons butter
- ½ cup flour
- 2 cups red wine
- 28 ounces canned Italian peeled tomatoes
- 2 cups Chicken Stock (page 214)
- 1 cup quartered large button mushrooms
- 4 ounces dried porcini mushrooms, soaked in 2 ounces (¼ cup) very hot water to soften

- Add porcini mushrooms (sliced, if the pieces are very large) along with their soaking liquid.
- Return the brisket to the pan and cover with the lid or aluminium foil.
- Place in the oven and braise gently for 2 to 3 hours, checking occasionally to make sure the liquid is not boiling. The meat should be very tender, almost "falling off the bone," and the sauce will have thickened slightly.
- Turn off the heat, but leave the pan undisturbed inside the oven for 30 minutes.
- Remove the meat to a cutting board, slice across the grain into thin slices, and arrange on a serving platter. Garnish with the sauce and vegetables from the pan and serve.

JUDY'S SUMMER TOMATOES
WITH CUCUMBER, ONION, BASIL, AND RED WINE VINEGAR

More than any other dish, this one reminds me of eating with my family when I was growing up. As children, we ate this salad all summer long (like it or not), and almost everything in it came from my mother's garden.

I don't want to sound like a Hallmark card, but if I close my eyes and let myself daydream a bit, I can just picture the scene: It's dusk, just before dinner, and I am already at my seat at the kitchen table. My mother, Judy, is walking from her garden toward the sliding backdoor that leads to the kitchen. She is carrying a wicker basket filled with juicy, ripe tomatoes, cucumbers, red onions, and basil. The gardening gloves she is wearing are stained with dirt, as she has just picked everything for the night's first course. I ask her, "What's for dinner?" as if I didn't know. I can't tell you how many times we started a meal this way, and the funny thing is, I still make this salad all the time. It is simple, delicious, and, for me, certainly nostalgic.

Happy, Mom?

- 4 very ripe beefsteak tomatoes, cut into medium dice
- 2 large ripe unpeeled cucumbers, halved lengthwise, then sliced into half-moons
- 1 red onion, thinly sliced
- 12 basil leaves, torn in large pieces
- 4 ounces (½ cup) extra-virgin olive oil
- 2 ounces (¼ cup) red wine vinegar

  Salt, pepper, and crushed red pepper flakes, to taste

Serves 4 to 6 as a first course

Pay attention, because if you blink, you are going to miss this one!
- One hour before dinner, put everything in a large mixing bowl.
- Toss and refrigerate.
- Serve.

TO MAKE AN AUTHENTIC TUSCAN PANZANELLA Dry out twenty cubes of Italian bread in a low oven until they are very hard, let them cool, then add them to this salad along with another ¼ cup good olive oil and eight torn mint leaves. I first encountered this classic salad while cooking at Sapore di Mare. The inventive, not to mention thrifty, addition of day-old Tuscan bread to the familiar ingredients from my mother's summer salad seemed a stroke of genius. The bread not only makes the salad more substantial, it also soaks up all the tasty juices. Unfortunately, once Italian American chain restaurants got a hold of this refreshing salad they couldn't leave well enough alone. I've seen it with just about everything in the kitchen thrown in, from garlic and seafood to sausages and peppers and back again. They may still call it *panzanella*, but no Tuscan would agree. Shame, shame . . .

SLOW-ROASTED SALMON
WITH CABBAGE, BACON, AND DILL

1 head savoy cabbage (¾ head regular green cabbage can be substituted)

6 slices bacon, cut into 6 to 8 pieces each

1 onion, cut into small dice

8 ounces (1 cup) water, plus additional if needed

4 6-ounce salmon fillets, skin removed

1 teaspoon chopped fresh dill, plus additional for garnish

2 ounces (4 tablespoons) extra-virgin olive oil, plus additional for drizzling over roasted fish

4 small knobs butter (a "knob" is about 1 teaspoon)

Juice of 1 lemon

Salt and pepper

Try cooking salmon like this, and you might never cook it any other way again. The low-temperature oven really does improve the texture of the fish. The combination of salmon, cabbage, and bacon is perfect for cooler weather, making this an ideal meal for fall, but it's great anytime. For a hearty variation, add some diced, blanched potatoes to the cabbage as it finishes braising.

Makes dinner for 4

- Halve the cabbage lengthwise, cut out the core, then remove the leaves and slice them into 2½-inch squares.
- Preheat the oven to 250°F.
- Place the bacon in a medium sauce pot over medium heat. Render the bacon until cooked but not crispy. You should have approximately 2 ounces (4 tablespoons) fat; if you have more, discard the excess.
- Add the onion and sauté for 1 minute.
- Add the cabbage and water and let simmer uncovered until the cabbage is tender, about 15 minutes. If all the water evaporates during cooking, add more as needed until the cabbage is very tender.
- Meanwhile, place the salmon fillets on a nonstick sheet pan. Drizzle 1 table-spoon of the olive oil over each fillet. Season with salt, pepper, and half the dill. Top each fillet with a knob of butter and place in the oven. Cook 15 to 18 minutes for medium rare, 21 to 24 minutes for medium (depending on the thickness of the fish), and if you cook it any longer than that, I can't be held responsible.
- When the cabbage is meltingly soft and tender, season with salt, pepper, and the rest of the dill. Keep warm while the salmon finishes cooking.
- Remove the salmon from the oven and drizzle with the lemon juice.

TO SERVE
- Divide the cabbage between four dinner plates, top with the salmon fillets, and drizzle a little more olive oil over the fish.
- Season with freshly ground pepper, sprinkled on and around the fish.
- Garnish with additional fresh dill, if desired, and serve.

EVERYONE NEEDS RULES. . . . When you were a kid, didn't it sometimes seem like the world was out to get you? Like some higher being was pulling strings just to mess with your existence, trying to teach you a life lesson that you did not necessarily want to learn? For me, that higher being was my father, Ned.

When I was about 13 years old, my father suddenly imposed the "Rules of the Kitchen" on our household. My father is a very compassionate, fair-minded man, so this seemed like a rather drastic measure; I realize now that he had no choice. Simply put, my siblings and I drove him to it.

Over the years we had somehow become a pretty freewheeling bunch as far as food was concerned. We remembered our table manners, of course, and we were always respectful of our elders, but we'd been on a downward slope for quite a while when it came to preparing our own snacks and cleaning up after ourselves. In particular, we'd fallen into the awful habit of leaving food all over the place. Peanut butter crackers in the playroom, half-eaten tuna sandwiches under our beds or in my father's office. My father would find these "traces" and go ballistic, although at the time I sure couldn't see what all the fuss was about.

My father is an attorney, and he crafted his kitchen rules like a true legislator. He must have worked on them for weeks, weaving new sanitary regulations and guidelines for more peaceful family dinners into his manifesto, and thinking up new chores for us while he was at it. I thought he had it in for me. I already had plenty of homework and my younger siblings to deal with, why did he want to ruin my life even further and come up with these silly rules?

Once his decree went into effect, I felt like I'd been tied up in a straitjacket, and I wanted desperately to break free. But he was the general, and as the privates in his army, we had no choice but to fall in. Believe me, his ways were going to win out over our objections.

Funny thing is, with time I relented and accepted; I even started to enjoy the new format. My father had a higher understanding, a game plan for what we needed so we would be able to cope with all of life's little obstacles. He knew what was best for us. He knew at that point in our lives we needed a little structure; he knew that sometimes everyone needs rules.

NED'S RULES OF THE KITCHEN

1 No eating out of the kitchen until after age 30. (When I turned 27 and thought I was closing in on my dining freedom, Ned upped the age to 35.)

2 No television during dinner.

3 No telephone during dinner. (Ned answered the phone every time it rang at the dinner hour and told our friends when they could call back.)

4 The children are responsible for clearing the table. (One week in three it was my turn to clear everyone's plate and then return to my seat for an additional ten minutes of "family conversation.")

5 The children shall restore order to the kitchen after meals. (One week out of three, the kitchen was my duty. The sink had to be cleaned, the floor swept, and the dishwasher emptied. If my brother or sister attempted sabotage and dirtied up the place on my guard, I was still held accountable.)

6 The children are responsible for emptying the garbage. (Every third week I had to make sure it was taken out.)

7 There is only one dinner. Special orders will be accepted only on birthdays, when the birthday-boy or -girl may choose the entire menu. (As the evil older brother, I always picked something my brother and sister couldn't stand.)

8 As a corollary to Rule 7, no dish served at mealtime may be refused. (We had to try everything that was served. At least try a bite. Then, if we really did not like it, special dispensation might possibly be granted.)

9 Dinner is served promptly at 7:00 P.M. (We were to be home and in our seats for dinner. No excuses.)

10 No fighting at the table. (Ever.)

11 Friends are welcome to stay for dinner. (Always, anytime.)

YUKON GOLD POTATO SOUP
WITH SHRIMP, BACON, AND POTATOES

FOR THE SOUP

4 very large Yukon Gold potatoes, peeled and cut into medium dice

1 white onion, peeled and cut into medium dice

1 large celery root, peeled and cut into medium dice

1 leek, white part only, thinly sliced

1 quart Clear Vegetable Stock (page 214)

3 quarts whole milk

8 ounces (1 cup) crème fraîche

2 tablespoons butter

Salt and white pepper

FOR THE GARNISH (PER SERVING)

2 medium shrimp, shelled

1 slice smoked bacon, diced

1 tablespoon diced Yukon Gold potatoes

A few pinches of finely sliced chives

Small pinch of kosher salt

Freshly ground black pepper

My father, Ned, is crazy for soup, and this is one of his favorites. It bears a striking resemblance to a chowder, but it's more elegant. For a special touch, you can dress it up even more (for instance, when the kids are at a sleepover) by replacing the shrimp and bacon garnish with some chopped cooked lobster and a dollop of caviar. Pour a couple glasses of champagne, light some romantic candles, and hope the kids don't get homesick.

TRUC If you need to hurry this recipe along, cut the vegetables a bit smaller and they will cook faster. Don't do anything crazy like puree the vegetables before making the soup, it just won't work — trust me, I tried it once.

NOTE The garnish and soup can both be prepared a day ahead.

DEFINITELY NOTE Since I thought you might like to have extra soup around, the garnish listed below is per bowl. Multiply accordingly depending on how many people you will be serving. Figure around 6 ounces (¾ cup) soup per person for a first course.

Makes 4 quarts (leftovers freeze well)

FOR THE SOUP

- Place potatoes, onion, celery root, leek, vegetable stock, and milk in a large soup pot and cook gently over medium heat until the potatoes and celery root are tender, about 30 minutes.
- Remove from heat, let cool slightly, and puree in batches in a high-speed blender until smooth and creamy.
- Return soup to pot and stir in the crème fraîche and butter.
- Add salt and white pepper, to taste.

FOR THE GARNISH

- Bring a medium sauce pot full of lightly salted water to a boil.
- Add the shrimp, lower the heat, and simmer until the shrimp are pink and cooked through.
- Let cool, slice into half-inch pieces, and set aside.
- Render bacon over low heat until just crispy and drain on paper towels.
- Blanch the diced potatoes in salted, boiling water until just tender. Drain and set aside.
- Just before serving, combine shrimp, bacon, and potatoes and season with salt and pepper.

TO SERVE

- Gently reheat the soup over low heat.
- Place the shrimp, bacon, and potato mixture in warmed soup bowls.
- Pour the soup over the top, garnish with the chives and freshly ground black pepper, and serve.

THE KITCHEN IS NO PLACE TO PLAY GAMES My mother has some kind of crazy, unspoken competition going on in her kitchen. It's not *Iron Chef* or *Ready, Set, Cook*, but it's a competition nonetheless, and I call it *Need an Ingredient?*

Now, my mother keeps a ridiculous amount of food in the house, even though she and my father are the only ones at home, and it has been years since all the kids moved away. I think this need to have an absurdly overstocked pantry could trace back to my grandparents, who lived through the Depression, or else it grew out of times in our own family life when we had difficulty making ends meet and it was a chore to put food on the table. But if a nuclear war broke out today, my mother's kitchen is where you'd want to be, in her pantry to be exact. Ask my mother for an ingredient. Go ahead, ask her for anything, and 99 times out of 100, she'll have it. The woman has a mini-supermarket in her house!

When I visit my parents I usually get roped into cooking at least one meal. No big deal, I love to cook, and I'm happy to do it for them. I always give this meal a great deal of thought, because I want to prepare them something special, something they'll really enjoy. I might say, "Mom, I'd like to make you this new appetizer from our spring menu. I know you guys would love it, but the dish calls for hijinki and topiko." She remains unfazed. "Michael," she says with that certain deadpan confidence only mothers have, "I have both of them in the freezer! And by the way, which type of topiko do you want, regular orange or wasabi infused?"

I am not kidding! She's a show-off! How many mothers keep hijinki in the freezer just in case someone needs it? She takes it personally on the rare occasion that she can't fulfill a request; in fact, she gets truly depressed. Or else she lies. "Oh, I just used the last of the yuzu juice, I'll get some more tomorrow." And if you stump her with dried wood-ear mushrooms, you can bet she'll have a package in the pantry by your next visit, which of course she'll show you the minute you walk in the door. The hellos and welcome may be abbreviated. She'll eventually get around to parading you upstairs to see the new wallpaper in the guest bedroom, but the mushrooms, well, they are far more important and newsworthy to her than any cosmetic changes she may have made to her house!

CREAMY CHICKEN STEW

WITH VEGETABLES THAT ARE SUPPOSED TO BE GOOD FOR YOU

Why is it so hard to get kids to eat things that are green? Why just that color? Kids will eat things that are red (tomato sauce) or brown (cookies and brownies) or even white (paste). But there seems to be some sort of innate aversion to the color green when it comes to food. Are the adults to blame?

When I asked my friend Stuart's four-year-old daughter about this, she said, "Well, you know, maybe it's just not their favorite color." I guess not. So I left as many green things out of this as possible, and with any luck you'll have no problem convincing your kids to eat it.

Makes dinner for 4

- Heat the olive oil in a large, high-sided pan over a high flame.
- Season the chicken with salt and pepper, add to the pan, and sear until golden brown, about 2 minutes.
- Remove from the pan with a slotted spoon and set aside.
- Add the butter and melt over high heat.
- Add the sage leaves, cook 1 minute, then remove and discard.
- Add all of the vegetables, stir to coat, and sauté for 1 to 2 minutes.
- Sprinkle in the flour and reduce the heat to medium. Stir to coat the vegetables evenly and cook for 1 to 2 minutes.
- Pour in the stock and the milk, stirring constantly until fully incorporated.
- Return the chicken to the pot and simmer with the vegetables 20 to 30 minutes on low heat, until vegetables are tender and stew has thickened.
- Taste for seasoning, adding more salt and pepper if needed.
- Serve with Buttered "Noodles" (see next page).

3 ounces (6 tablespoons) extra-virgin olive oil

4 large boneless, skinless chicken breasts, cut into 1-inch cubes

Salt and pepper

3 tablespoons butter

4 fresh sage leaves

8 large button mushrooms, quartered

1 large carrot, peeled, halved lengthwise, and sliced into ⅛-inch-thick half-moons

12 pearl onions, peeled and blanched for 2 minutes

8 Brussels sprouts, trimmed, quartered, and blanched for 4 minutes

1 cup cauliflower, cut into florets

1 celery stalk, cut into ⅛-inch-thick pieces

½ cup flour

1½ quarts Chicken Stock (page 214)

8 ounces (1 cup) milk

BUTTERED "NOODLES"

WITH PARMIGIANO-REGGIANO AND SAGE

1 pound ditalini pasta

8 tablespoons butter, cut into 6 pieces

8 large fresh sage leaves, chopped

Salt and pepper

¼ cup grated Parmigiano-Reggiano cheese

I make this for myself all the time. It is great as an accompaniment to Creamy Chicken Stew (page 43) but it can also stand on its own. I like to use ditalini (small tubes) because they cook quickly, are fun to eat, and are reminiscent of "mac and cheese." (I'm still working that kid angle.) For grown-ups you can use fettuccine, and maybe you'll even make them feel nostalgic — stew with buttered noodles, just like Mom used to make. You can also serve the butter sauce with ravioli, agnolotti, gnocchi — even crepes stuffed with mushrooms and hazelnuts.

NOTE If you have to remove green things from your kids' food, leave the sage leaves whole and remove them before you put the pasta in.

Makes 4 to 6 side dishes

- Bring a large pot of lightly salted water to a boil.
- Add the pasta to the boiling water, stir to keep from sticking, and cook for 10 minutes or so, until al dente.
- Meanwhile, melt the butter in a large sauce pot over high heat until it starts to foam and turn a light golden brown.
- Add the sage leaves and a few pinches of salt and pepper.
- Ladle 3 ounces (6 tablespoons) of the pasta water into the butter and sage mixture and remove from heat.
- When the pasta is cooked, strain and transfer to the sauce pot. Toss with the butter mixture to blend.
- Add the cheese, and adjust seasoning if needed. The sauce should just coat the pasta; if it seems too soupy, wait a minute or so and the pasta will absorb the liquid.
- Serve on its own, or with your favorite braised meats or stews.

LOIN OF PORK "À L'APICIUS"

Does this sound like a fancy dish, or what?

Relax — it just sounds fancy. I make this all of the time at my house and even at guest-chef events, because people really seem to enjoy the balanced seasoning of sweet, spicy, tart, and aromatic.

Since you already have an audience sitting around the dinner table, and you are discussing everything from politics to history, I thought I would give you the history part of the conversation. Your family will really be impressed; in fact, they will suggest you audition for *Jeopardy* someday soon.

Apicius was a Roman chef and bon vivant whose first cookbook only contained sauces. (I wonder how he ever got that idea past his agent!) He liked to experiment with his cooking and created dishes using nightingales' tongues and camels' heels, among other oddities. These dishes were apparently meant to startle the complacent citizenry, but other interesting things came out of it: The historian Pliny credits Apicius with the idea of force-feeding geese to enlarge their livers, some of our very first foie gras!

Apicius eventually went broke and committed suicide to save his pride, but now you can enjoy his roast pork loin and do your part to help his legacy live on. You can serve this with just about anything — roasted potatoes, rice of any kind, or just vegetables.

1 cup honey

4 ounces (½ cup) red wine vinegar

1 teaspoon curry powder

¼ teaspoon cayenne pepper

2 ounces (4 tablespoons) canola oil

1 center loin of pork, trimmed of any excess fat (about 3 pounds, 6 inches in diameter)

Salt and pepper

4 ounces (½ cup) water

3 to 4 ounces (6 to 8 tablespoons) Chicken Stock (page 214; water can be substituted)

2 tablespoons butter

Makes 6 dinner-sized portions

- Heat the oven to 300°F.
- Mix the honey, vinegar, curry powder, and cayenne pepper in a bowl and set aside.
- Place a large, ovenproof pan on the stove over medium heat and add the canola oil.
- Season the pork liberally with salt and pepper and place in the pan.
- Cook pork gently, just 30 seconds per side, to obtain a light change in color. Do not sear.
- Pour the honey mixture over the pork.
- Pour the water into the bottom of the pan, taking care not to pour it on the pork.
- Place the pan in the oven and roast for 1 hour, turning the pork and basting it with the pan juices every 3 to 5 minutes.
- Turn the oven off.
- Remove the pork from the pan, place on a baking sheet, and return it to the oven to stay warm, about 10 minutes, while you prepare the sauce.

directions are continued on following page

- Transfer the pan juices to a medium-sized sauce pot.
- Add the chicken stock or water to the sauce pot and reduce over medium heat until about ½ cup remains.
- Swirl in the butter, stirring until melted, and remove from heat.
- Remove the pork from the oven and carve into thick slices. Arrange on a platter, drizzle the sauce over the top, and serve.

BROCCOLINI
WITH SPICY SOY AND ORANGE ZEST

3 ounces (6 tablespoons) water

Juice and zest of 1 orange

2 bunches broccolini, rubber band removed

1 shallot, peeled and sliced into thin rings

2 ounces (4 tablespoons) extra-virgin olive oil, plus extra for garnish

1 ounce (2 tablespoons) good quality, low-sodium soy sauce

¼ teaspoon togarashi (see note on page 24; cayenne pepper can be substituted)

Salt, if needed

Black pepper, for garnish

Broccolini, a cross between Chinese broccoli and Chinese kale, is a relative newcomer to the produce aisle, and I've become a great fan of it, both for cooking at home and in my restaurants. Effortless to prepare, quick to cook, hardly any waste, and rumor has it it's even good for you (don't tell your kids!). I had often wanted to offer a standing ovation to the genius who created it. Then one day my former chef de cuisine, Brian Reimer, brought his father, Jerry, to dinner at Radius. We got to talking, naturally about food, and the subject turned to vegetables — the ones we love and the ones we could do without. Turns out Brian's father works for Sakata, the seed company that invented and trademarked broccolini! Although much of the science is lost on me, I've always marveled at the ingenuity required to create hybrid vegetables. Who decides what vegetables to match up? What determines whether a pairing will work or not? Mr. Reimer told me a few amazing stories about vegetable mutations too gruesome to describe in this wholesome, family-oriented book.

Makes 4 side dishes

- Place the water and the orange juice in a sauce pot large enough to hold the broccolini. Cover and bring to a boil over high heat.
- Add the broccolini, cover, and cook for 3 minutes. Shake the pan occasionally to coat the broccolini thoroughly with the liquid.
- Remove cover and let liquid reduce until almost gone, but not completely dry.
- Add the shallot, olive oil, soy sauce, togarashi, and orange zest, and stir well to combine.
- Test the broccolini for doneness. I prefer it fairly crunchy, not soft and mushy, but that's just me.
- Adjust the seasoning, adding more togarashi or salt, if needed. There should be a hint of spice and salt.
- Transfer to a platter, grind some black pepper on top, add a drizzle of olive oil if you like, and serve.

GRILLED FENNEL SAUSAGES
WITH PEPPERS, ONIONS, AND POTATOES

4 large red bliss potatoes, sliced into ½-inch rounds

4 ounces (½ cup) extra-virgin olive oil

½ clove garlic, thinly sliced

2 large red peppers, cored, seeded, and cut into julienne strips

2 ounces (¼ cup) water

1 large white onion, thinly sliced

8 really good-quality sweet fennel sausages

1 pinch fresh rosemary, chopped

1 teaspoon capers, soaked in cold water for a few minutes

20 to 25 whole Italian parsley leaves

Salt and pepper

I love stuff like this for dinner. This is a rustic, satisfying dish that can be prepared with very little trouble — perfect for a family supper. As with so many simple recipes, success hinges on the quality of the ingredients, so ask your butcher for help in selecting the finest sausage available. If you do not want to grill the sausages, they can be seared in a sauté pan.

NOTE The Sautéed Broccoli Rabe (page 69) goes perfectly with this.

Dinner for 4

- Turn your grill to high and preheat your oven to 500°F.
- Toss the potato slices with 2 ounces (¼ cup) of the olive oil, arrange on a nonstick sheet pan, and roast in oven until golden brown and tender, about 20 minutes. (Open the oven and give them a stir about halfway through the cooking time.)
- Meanwhile, put remaining olive oil and sliced garlic in a large sauté pan and cook over high heat until the garlic is golden brown.
- Add the peppers and cook 4 to 5 minutes, until they start to soften.
- Add the water to the pan.
- Add the onion and sauté until the peppers and onion are tender, 5 minutes or so, then keep warm while you cook the sausages.
- Split the sausages lengthwise and press gently to flatten.
- Put the sausages on the grill and let them char slightly on both sides for 2 to 3 minutes.
- Lower the heat to medium or move sausages to a cooler part of the grill and cook until done, 10 more minutes. Turn once or twice to cook evenly.
- When the potatoes are crispy and browned, remove them from the oven and add to the pepper and onion mixture.
- Add the rosemary and capers to the pepper and onion mixture and season with salt and pepper.
- Toss in the parsley and keep the mixture warm while the sausages finish cooking.
- Transfer the vegetable mixture to a platter, put the sausages on top, and serve.

SECRET AGENT RASPBERRY BARS

I can't tell you why these are called secret agent raspberry bars without putting my life in jeopardy; I know it all sounds very cloak and dagger. Still, the name alone will ensure your kids love helping you make these bars. What I can tell you is that my sister-in-law, Sue, gave me the recipe, and it is next to impossible to eat just one. When I am placed in charge of these, I cut the squares even bigger. Then I can still say, "I was good, I only ate two."

¾ cup softened butter

½ cup sugar

1¾ cups flour

⅓ cup chopped pecans

¼ teaspoon almond extract

¼ teaspoon salt

8 ounces (1 cup) seedless raspberry preserves

½ cup sweetened, flaked coconut

Makes about 30 squares

- Preheat oven to 350°F.
- Using a mixer, beat together butter and sugar at medium speed.
- Add flour and mix well.
- Add chopped pecans, almond extract, and salt, stirring until the flour mixture resembles coarse crumbs.
- Reserve 1 cup of the flour mixture and press the remainder into the bottom of an ungreased 9 x 13-inch baking dish.
- Spread raspberry preserves evenly over the crust.
- Sprinkle the reserved flour mixture over the preserves.
- Sprinkle the coconut over the top.
- Bake until the crust and topping are golden, 25 to 30 minutes.
- Let cool and cut into squares.
- In the unlikely event there are any leftovers, store in an airtight container.

Chapter 3

TIME TO PAY A LITTLE RESPECT

SCENES FROM AN ITALIAN RESTAURANT

I really get up on my soapbox when it comes to authentic Italian food, like a street preacher on the Boston Common or, more aptly, like an orator on some balustrade in ancient Rome.

I was born in Brooklyn and went to high school in central New Jersey, two places with strong Italian communities. So I really thought I'd grown up around absolutely authentic Italian food. Many of the people I knew spoke something that certainly sounded like Italian, and their parents and grandparents seemed intent on preserving what I could only imagine was the legitimate article when it came to things like cooking, language, and customs.

Back then, I thought asking for a spoon for my spaghetti meant I was "in the know" just like Robert De Niro and Bruno Kirby in the pasta scene from *The Godfather II*. I thought grated cheese went on everything and there was garlic in every Italian recipe. I said *muzzarell* for mozzarella, *galamar* for calamari. And pasta e fagioli and proscuitto were *pastafajul* and *pershoot*, respectively. What I didn't know was that in standard Italian every letter in the word is enunciated.

So my first day working at Sapore di Mare, Pino Luongo's Tuscan restaurant in Wainscott, New York, was nothing short of an eye-opening experience. I think back on those early months and I just know the Italians in the kitchen, direct from places like Sardinia, Rome, and Arezzo, must have laughed behind my back as I butchered their language.

My verbal gaffes were on par with my culinary miscues. I remember going to Pino's office in New York City for a menu development meeting. I had come armed with some of my own ideas for twists on dishes he had catalogued over the years. There were certain dishes on the Sapore di Mare menu that were staples, and I was about to learn they were just not to be messed with.

I brought up his classic rigatoni dish, tossed with sausage, peas, tomatoes, and cream, and Pino asked, "How are you going to improve on that?" Then I launched into a well-rehearsed speech about a new idea of mine, and how I could . . .

I was cut down immediately. His question was a rhetorical one. What he was trying to tell me, although I was not hearing his question, was this: How could you possibly improve this rigatoni recipe? It does not need your meddling. It does not need you to do anything but re-create it over and over again. Perfectly.

From that point on, I learned that creating great Italian food is really about two things: honoring tradition and cooking simply with products that are as local and fresh as possible. The cuisines of Italy are based on longstanding tradition, and many an argument has been fought over which region, province, city, or town makes the best _____. You fill in the blank; Italians like to argue over everything. To complicate matters further, a common misconception is that Italian cooking is broken into two categories, Northern and Southern. It is actually divided into 20 or 21 regions (again, depending on who is counting, and arguing). Each one offers a very unique and distinctive cuisine.

I now understand Pino was not telling me that new recipes cannot be created; he just wanted me to pay real respect to the old ones. They've become classics for a reason and may not need any "creativity" to make them better.

Simplicity first; that is the real Italian way.

With Via Matta, my business partner, Christopher Myers, and I set out to build an original, urban restaurant that would serve authentic Italian food in downtown Boston. This turned out to be easier said than done. When the restaurant was still in its planning stages, I spoke to my friend Mario Batali about the regional cuisines we wanted to feature on the menu. "Do we need some sort of catch to this place?" I asked.

He said, "Be Italian!"

I said, "Well, we are cooking Italian."

"Yeah, but be Italian, and cook with as many local products as you can. That's what Italians do; they cook what they can see from their homes. Be inspired and create your menu based on what your local fishermen and farmers have to offer."

We took his sage advice. The guests at Via Matta have really taken to the classic, simply prepared dishes we serve. They tell us they feel like they're eating in Italy, which is exactly what we set out to accomplish, and we could not be happier. We use as many fresh regional products as possible, and I suggest you do the same at home.

I love all things Italian — the food, people, history, language, style. I could talk about Italian culture for days. But since this isn't strictly an Italian cookbook, let's just say *to be continued. . . .*

PENNE ALL'ARRABBIATA

Food can do many things for us. A bowl of *penne all'arrabbiata* once helped get me a date with a girl who had lived and studied in Italy. I had just been hired at the restaurant where she was working, and she was playing hard to get. Basically, she had ignored me from the moment I walked in the door. Then one day she came into the kitchen and announced that she was starving. I asked what she wanted to eat, and she said she had something in mind, but I wouldn't know how to make it. "Try me," I told her. She rolled her eyes and replied, "Penne all'arrabbiata . . . but the real Italian way, not some American version." I told her to come back in ten minutes. When she returned, I presented her with the pasta, and it was exactly how she remembered it from her days in Italy. Next thing I knew, she had agreed to go out with me. The love affair didn't last, but our friendship and a mutual love for *penne all'arrabbiata* have endured all these years. Thank goodness for perfectly cooked pasta and whole Italian parsley! You'll notice this dish doesn't have any garlic or cheese, yet somehow it is still Italian.

NOTE *Arrabbiata* means "angry" in Italian, and it refers to the heat of the peppers in this dish. It is very spicy! Please do not adjust the seasoning; if you want something milder, I would suggest another dish.

ANOTHER NOTE To make milled tomatoes, which turn up often in this book, pass good-quality, canned whole Italian tomatoes and their juices through a hand-turned food mill. If you can find San Marzano tomatoes, they are the best.

Makes 2 generous portions

- Bring a large pot of salted water to a boil.
- Add the penne and cook for 7 to 9 minutes. Stir from time to time to keep the pasta from sticking.
- Heat the olive oil, salt, pepper, and crushed red pepper flakes in a large sauté pan for 1 minute over high heat.
- Add the milled tomatoes and cook over high heat for 8 to 10 minutes, until the tomatoes start to thicken and darken ever so slightly.
- When the pasta is al dente, strain and add to the sauce in the sauté pan.
- Cook the pasta and the sauce together for 1 to 2 minutes, until the pasta absorbs most of the sauce.
- Add the parsley leaves and toss for 30 seconds.
- Serve. Please don't pass the cheese — even though Americans tend to serve cheese on every pasta dish, Italians would cringe at the thought of using it with this one.

---

8 ounces penne rigate

4 ounces (½ cup) extra-virgin olive oil

4 pinches kosher salt

2 pinches black pepper

4 pinches crushed red pepper flakes

2½ cups milled Italian tomatoes

1 large handful whole Italian parsley leaves

PINO AND PASTA It was 1989 when I drove out to the Hamptons from New York City filled with anticipation and eager to start my new job at Sapore di Mare, Pino Luongo's authentic Tuscan restaurant in Wainscott. Finally, I thought, I am getting out of the city and living at the beach. What could be better? Spring was giving way to summer, and I would be manning the pasta station at the hottest restaurant in the Hamptons.

I thought I was well-versed for my new job. I had worked in Italian restaurants before, and I had certainly eaten in my share of what I thought were authentic Italian restaurants in New York City and New Jersey. I was sure I had all the moves down pat.

Traffic was heavy. Three hours and forty-five minutes after leaving New York City, I arrived at the restaurant's kitchen door. I was greeted by an old Italian woman named Maria who didn't speak a lick of English. Instead, she just sort of grunted and pointed to the main kitchen. Ah, just the beginning I had imagined. . . .

Walking into a busy restaurant kitchen in the middle of dinner service, unknown to the entire staff, is one of the most uncomfortable situations imaginable. Everyone is moving at a frenetic pace. The glances and glares you receive from the staff, the same people you will soon be spending 16 hours a day with, are enough to make you turn around and go back from wherever you just came.

Just before I allowed those stares to have any real effect, Pino, my new boss, spotted me and offered a warm, gregarious welcome. "Mark, Mark, so good to have you here."

"Actually, my name is Michael," I replied.

"Right . . . you must be starving. How was your ride out from the city?"

"Fine."

"Hido, make Mark something to eat."

"Michael, my name is . . ."

"Right, Michael, Michael. Make Michael something to eat. *Spaghetti aglio e olio con pomodoro. Subito!*"

I didn't speak much Italian, but I knew enough to understand that Pino had just ordered me a bowl of pasta with olive oil, garlic, and tomato. "What a cheapskate," I thought. That's what my mother made when she was trying to save money. I had just spent almost four hours getting to the restaurant, and that's all he had to offer? Not exactly the warm welcome I had envisioned. Where was the shrimp scampi? Where were the clams casino?

I was shown to a small table right smack in the middle of the kitchen. I would eventually learn the table was reserved for "family," even though there was barely enough room for two people. Six minutes later, Pino brought me the most perfect bowl of pasta I had ever seen, let alone eaten. Words cannot describe the taste sensations I experienced at that moment, but I knew that bowl of spaghetti had just become the new standard against which all pastas would be judged. The sauce and pasta had become one, neither overpowering the other. The seasoning was expertly balanced, just the right amount of salt, spice, acid, and sweetness. And it tasted better and better with every bite.

Pino stopped to ask if everything was okay. I nodded through my delirium, and asked if I could please have some cheese and a spoon for twirling my pasta onto my fork. He stopped dead in his tracks and looked at me dumbfounded. He was silent for a moment, and then simply replied in his heavy Italian accent, "Boy, this is your first day, don't make it your last." And with that, he turned and walked away.

Shortly after starting my new job, I learned that most Italians, especially Florentines, would never consider using a spoon to eat their pasta; they think it's close to blasphemy. And cheese on this particular dish (as well as many others) was just plain ole taboo.

I polished off my amazing *spaghetti aglio e olio con pomodoro*, and Pino silently approached me with an espresso. He handed it to me and stared as I gazed at the textbook *crema* floating on the coffee's surface. It was beautiful, but I could not help notice something was missing: Where was the lemon peel I had always been served before? Pino continued to glare in anticipation. Without a word, I took a sip. Don't question, don't ask, I thought. Best to just enjoy it, and ask someone else to explain things to me later. It was my first day. I did not want it to be my last.

CROSTINI OF CREAMY MUSHROOMS
WITH LEMON AND MINT

1 egg yolk

1 ounce (⅛ cup) water

Juice of half a lemon

1 teaspoon chopped fresh mint

½ teaspoon chopped
Italian parsley

1 heaping tablespoon flour

3 ounces (6 tablespoons)
extra-virgin olive oil

1 teaspoon butter

2 cups thinly sliced
button mushrooms

Salt and pepper

12 slices day-old Italian bread
(each piece should be 3 to 4
inches wide and ¾-inch thick)

¼ cup grated Parmigiano-
Reggiano cheese

Crostini are slices of Italian bread that have been drizzled with olive oil, toasted in the oven, and then topped with any of a variety of ingredients — from chicken livers to white bean puree. The oven-toasting is what distinguishes them from their cousin, the bruschetta, where sliced bread is grilled over an open flame then brushed with olive oil and possibly a little garlic. It's dishes like this that make me love Italian cooking: almost foolproof, tastes great, and very versatile — the mushroom topping is also excellent on grilled meats such as veal chops or steak. I could easily make a dinner out of nothing more than assorted crostini or bruschetta. So much for all those low-carb diets.

NOTE The best crostini and bruschetta are made from day-old bread.

Makes 12 crostini

- Preheat the oven to 450°F.
- Lightly beat the egg yolk and water in a small bowl or cup.
- Add the lemon juice, mint, parsley, and flour. Whisk until smooth and creamy.
- Heat 2 tablespoons olive oil with the butter in a medium saucepan over high heat.
- Add the mushrooms and sauté for 1 minute.
- Season with salt and pepper and cook until the mushrooms begin to release their liquid, about 3 minutes.
- Remove from the heat and let cool slightly, about 2 minutes.
- Arrange the bread slices on a baking sheet, drizzle with the remaining olive oil, and toast in the oven until golden brown on both sides.
- Pour the egg mixture over the slightly cooled mushrooms and cook gently over very low heat, stirring constantly, until the topping becomes creamy and thickened, about 2 minutes. Taste and adjust the seasoning.
- Remove the crostini from the oven.
- Spoon the mushroom mixture onto the crostini, garnish with a dusting of Parmigiano-Reggiano, and serve.

VONGOLE IN BRODETTO
(CLAMS IN BROTH)

3 ounces (6 tablespoons) extra-virgin olive oil

½ clove garlic, thinly sliced

Salt, pepper, and crushed red pepper flakes

20 to 24 top neck or cockle clams, cleaned (smaller is better — large clams are too tough; littleneck or mahogany clams may be substituted)

2 ounces (¼ cup) white wine

2 ounces (¼ cup) water

1 pinch fresh thyme leaves (optional)

1 tablespoon roughly chopped Italian parsley

See page 62 for how to clean clams

I don't have an addictive personality: drinking, drugs, and bettin' on the ponies have never been important to me. However, there is one thing I cannot seem to refrain from, and that is dipping my bread into soups, sauces, and stews. I am addicted to dipping. It may be harmless, but I'm guilty as charged! I just can't seem to help myself.

My mother used to yell at me for this. She would be making dinner and I would get a hunk of bread and stand over her stove and start dipping into whatever she was cooking. I never paid any attention to her constant cries of "Get outta there! Dinner will be ready in a few minutes! I don't want bread crumbs in my stew." I just kept dipping the bread in. I don't think that whole "double-dipping" thing was something any of us even considered back then; we had to wait for Seinfeld to coin the term for us.

NOTE The juices released by the clams flavor the sauce for some ultimate dipping, so canned clams are strictly banned from this recipe.

ANOTHER NOTE Choose a lidded, deep sauce pot for steaming the clams. They should not come more than halfway up the sides of the pan.

TRUC To grill perfect bread, use day-old bread rather than fresh. Preheat the grill to high, and when the rack is good and hot, lower the heat to medium. Drizzle the bread with extra-virgin olive oil before placing it on the grill. Grill the bread until each side is lightly charred.

Makes 2 first courses

- Place the olive oil and garlic in a medium sauce pot and cook over high heat until the garlic is golden brown.
- Add a small pinch each of salt, black pepper, and crushed red pepper flakes.
- Add the clams, white wine, water, and the thyme (if you are using it).
- Cover and cook over high heat until all of the clams open, shaking the pot once or twice to allow the clams room enough to open.
- Taste the broth for seasoning and adjust with more salt, pepper, or crushed red pepper flakes, if needed.
- Throw in the chopped parsley, divide everything between two bowls, and serve with plenty of grilled bread.

ON CLEANING CLAMS Nobody likes to eat sand, this I am sure of. Since clams insist on burying themselves in it, they have to be purged of all that irritating grit before they can be enjoyed to their fullest. Here is a really slick trick to make them spit out their sand before they are cooked: Add a few capfuls of vinegar to about 3 quarts of cold water in a deep bowl and submerge the clams for 10 to 15 minutes. Use plain white vinegar; it's cheap, and clams aren't particular. You'll be amazed how much sand they can give off, and grateful it didn't end up in your dinner.

RED SNAPPER

WITH BLACK OLIVES, CAPERS, AND TOMATO

I know it is hard to find real red snapper these days, but its unique flavor and texture — slightly oily and meaty, yet still flaky — make it worth seeking out for this preparation. Swordfish, tuna (grilled rare), grouper, or other firm-fleshed fish would make fine substitutes. To replicate an authentic meal along the Italian coast, invite some friends and eat outdoors. Have plenty of well-chilled white wine on hand.

NOTE Consider serving the snapper whole: head, tail, and all. Just throw it on the grill or roast it in the oven. A 6-pound fish will feed four, and take about 20 minutes on the grill. Even though fish might seem more tricky to eat this way, any Italian worth his salt will tell you that a whole cooked fish really does have more flavor than fillets.

ANOTHER NOTE Pitting the olives is really the only labor required for this recipe. Crunchy String Bean Salad with Red Onion and Prosciutto (page 90), served warm, rounds out this meal perfectly.

Makes 4 entrées

- Combine the olives, capers, red onion, tomatoes, basil, parsley, and olive oil in a mixing bowl.
- Season with salt, pepper, and a small pinch of crushed red pepper, and set aside at room temperature for 20 to 30 minutes before dinner.
- Use a very sharp knife to score a diagonal crosshatch in the skin side of the snapper fillets, cutting just through the skin and making the slits ½-inch apart.
- Split the 4 ounces (½ cup) canola oil between two large sauté pans and heat for 1 minute over high heat.
- Season the red snapper with salt and pepper on the skin side only and place skin-side down in the hot pans.
- Cook until the skin is a rich golden brown, about 3 minutes, lowering heat if necessary to keep the skin from becoming too dark.
- Season the top side of the fish with salt and pepper and flip the fillets over with a spatula.
- Remove from heat, but allow the fillets to remain in the pan.
- Let fish rest 3 minutes — fillets should be just cooked through — then squeeze the lemon juice around the fish and swirl the pan to combine.
- Transfer the fillets to dinner plates and garnish with spoonfuls of the tomato-olive mixture.
- Drizzle a spoonful of the pan juices over each fillet, garnish with whole parsley leaves, and serve.

8 to 10 black olives, rinsed, pitted, and roughly chopped (choose salt-cured olives, such as Gaeta or Kalamata)

1 teaspoon capers, rinsed briefly under cold water

1 tablespoon finely diced red onion

3 ripe plum tomatoes, cut into medium dice

4 large basil leaves, roughly chopped

1 tablespoon roughly chopped Italian parsley

2 ounces (¼ cup) extra-virgin olive oil

Salt, pepper, and crushed red pepper flakes

4 6-ounce pieces red snapper fillet, skin left on

4 ounces (½ cup) canola oil

Juice of 1 lemon

A few whole leaves of Italian parsley, for garnish

RIGATONI

WITH SOPPRESSATA, WHITE BEANS, TOMATO, AND BLACK OLIVES

8 ounces rigatoni

2 ounces (¼ cup) extra-virgin olive oil

3 tablespoons finely diced soppressata

1 pinch fresh rosemary, chopped

Salt, pepper, and crushed red pepper flakes

2 cups milled tomatoes (see note on page 55)

½ cup cooked white cannellini beans (canned can be substituted, but freshly cooked dried beans are best; see page 13 for notes on cooking beans)

10 Kalamata olives, rinsed in cold water, pitted, and quartered

4 tablespoons grated Parmigiano-Reggiano cheese

12 to 15 whole Italian parsley leaves

Once you have tasted this pasta dish the flavors have a way of haunting you in some peculiar way. I promise you will crave it on cold nights. It was taught to me by Salvo, a Sardinian man who was a master *pizzaiolo* (a person who specializes in making pizzas), a wonderful cook, and one of the best pranksters I have ever worked with. He truly knew how to have fun while he was at work. . . . even on the night the immigration and IRS agents stormed the restaurant looking for him. He managed to escape unscathed and returned to make a joke out of the situation. I don't want to get anyone in trouble, though, so that's all of the story I can divulge.

NOTE Soppressata is an aged Italian salami made from pork. It is slightly oily and smooth, though I've tasted homemade versions that were coarse-textured. The exact recipe varies from region to region, often including interesting flavor additions like fennel or hot red peppers. If you can't find it, hard Genoa salami would be a suitable substitute.

Makes 2 generous portions

- Bring a large pot of salted water to a boil.
- Add the rigatoni and boil 7 to 9 minutes, until al dente. Stir from time to time to keep rigatoni from sticking.
- Meanwhile, heat the olive oil in a large saucepan over high heat.
- Add the soppressata and fry for 1 minute.
- Add the rosemary and a pinch each of salt, pepper, and crushed red pepper flakes.
- Add the milled tomatoes and cook for 4 minutes.
- Stir in the white beans and olives.
- Cook for about 3 more minutes, until the sauce begins to thicken and turn a darker red. Remove the sauce from the heat if it appears cooked before the rigatoni is al dente. Check the pasta — it should be almost ready. When it is, strain the pasta and add it to the saucepan.
- Cook sauce and pasta together over high heat for 1 to 2 minutes, until the pasta absorbs most of the sauce.
- Check the seasoning, add the cheese and parsley leaves, toss for 30 seconds, and serve.

PAPPA AL POMODORO

(TUSCAN TOMATO AND BREAD SOUP)

This soup can only be made when tomatoes are at their best. Do not attempt to make this with anything other than really great, ripe tomatoes. Please heed my warning — I do not want to get any phone calls in the middle of the night complaining that this dish did not meet your expectations! With something this simple, this exposed, you really need to start with perfect ingredients at the height of their season.

NOTE I cook with several different varieties of extra-virgin olive oil, but you really need only two at home. One serves as a workhorse, an oil with plenty of body that will stand up to high heat during cooking. Then there is the extra-special oil, the rare one. It will cost you a little more money, but you will use less of it. A drizzle of truly fine oil over this *pappa al pomodoro* just before serving will add that extra bit of love you were looking for.

Makes 6 first courses

3 ounces (6 tablespoons) extra-virgin olive oil

½ clove garlic, sliced

8 ripe beefsteak tomatoes, cored and cut into medium dice

Salt

24 basil leaves, left whole

Black pepper and crushed red pepper flakes

10 1-inch cubes day-old Tuscan bread (should be very, very dry)

2 ounces (4 tablespoons) best-quality extra-virgin olive oil, for drizzling over soup

Parmigiano-Reggiano cheese, grated (optional)

- Heat the olive oil and sliced garlic together in a large sauce pot over medium heat until the garlic is golden brown.
- Add the tomatoes.
- Add a large pinch of salt (to help the tomatoes release their juices) and cook 5 to 7 minutes, until the tomatoes start to fall apart.
- Add basil leaves, black pepper, and crushed red pepper flakes, and continue cooking until the tomatoes are broken up, but have not dissolved completely, 3 to 5 more minutes.
- Taste, and add more salt, pepper, or crushed red pepper flakes, if needed.
- Remove from heat, add the dried bread cubes, and allow to cool for 30 minutes.
- Stir the soup with a wooden spoon to break the bread up slightly. Adjust seasoning again, if needed. The *pappa* should be slightly thick — not quite as dense as oatmeal, but not brothy either. This soup is best served warm, not piping hot.
- Portion the soup into six bowls, drizzle the olive oil (the really good stuff) on top, and serve. A sprinkling of Parmigiano is optional — I like to add it to this soup, but some Florentines would say No cheese.

GARLIC Boy, do Americans love garlic. Because it is such a powerful (and sometimes overpowering) ingredient, a few words on how, when, and where to use it really are in order.

First, I want to dispel the myth that garlic goes into every Italian dish. I don't know what led to this misconception, but somebody, somewhere, distorted the truth. There are countless Italian recipes that don't contain a hint of garlic, and in many recipes where garlic is listed as an ingredient it is never actually eaten. It is added to the pot with the other seasonings to flavor the dish and then discarded after it is cooked.

Second, garlic should be used just like salt and pepper. Unless it is listed in a recipe's name, like Spaghetti Aglio e Olio (spaghetti with garlic and olive oil), it is supposed to enhance the flavors of the other ingredients, not overwhelm them by means of some sort of hostile takeover. For perfectly cooked garlic, you can forget about mincing or using a garlic press. Both techniques lead to either raw or slightly burnt garlic, because it is next to impossible to cook those little tiny pieces perfectly and achieve the nutty, fragrant taste that garlic can contribute when cooked correctly. Instead, cut the clove into thin slices or smash it lightly by pressing down on it with the flat part of a knife. Don't heat the oil or butter before adding the garlic. Rather, put the garlic and oil or butter in an unheated pan, place over the burner, and cook until the garlic starts to turn a light golden brown. Then you can either remove it and cook with the flavored oil or proceed with the next step in your recipe.

Finally, chill out about the amount of garlic you use! Like cologne or perfume, a little goes a long way; everyone in your office does not need to know what you had for dinner last night.

SAUTÉED BROCCOLI RABE
WITH HOT RED PEPPER FLAKES

Broccoli rabe is my absolute favorite vegetable, hands-down, no contest. I like it with pasta, under grilled sausages, as a topping for bruschetta, on a pizza, or simply prepared like this, as a side dish.

NOTE Just because you respect your elders doesn't mean you can't occasionally suggest an innovation — especially when your proposition is designed to highlight something your elders already prize. Broccoli rabe has a bitter flavor that I love, and I've found that boiling it, as many old Italian recipes suggest, washes away much of that amazing punch. So I sauté broccoli rabe without blanching it first, which I think retains the integrity of the vegetable and allows you to enjoy it the way God intended. If you want something milder, buy spinach and prepare it the same way.

TRUC Cleaning broccoli rabe is very easy. Simply take a sharp knife and trim off the bottom three inches or so, leaving the leafy tops with a couple inches of stem. Chop roughly into slightly smaller pieces, and that's all you have to do.

Makes a contorno for 2 (or just for 1 if I am eating it)

- Place the olive oil and garlic in a sauce pot and cook over medium-high heat until the garlic starts to turn golden brown.
- Add two pinches of salt, one pinch of black pepper, and one pinch of crushed red pepper flakes.
- Add the broccoli rabe and sauté for 2 minutes
- Add the water, turn the heat up to high, and sauté 2 more minutes, or until tender.
- Taste for seasoning and serve.

2 ounces (¼ cup) extra-virgin olive oil

½ clove garlic, thinly sliced

Salt, pepper, and crushed red pepper flakes

1 head broccoli rabe, trimmed

2 ounces (¼ cup) water

CONTORNO *is Italian for "side dish." A contorno is meant to be ordered and shared, and just like the baked potato, coleslaw, or corn on the cob in American steak houses, it is ordered separately.*

OSSO BUCO
WITH GREMOLATA AND SAFFRON RISOTTO

FOR THE
OSSO BUCO

6 2-inch-thick veal shanks

Salt and pepper

About 1 cup all-purpose flour (3 to 5 tablespoons for thickening the sauce, plus additional for dredging the veal shanks)

3 ounces (6 tablespoons) extra-virgin olive oil

½ cup butter

½ clove garlic, thinly sliced

½ cup finely diced white onion

½ cup finely diced carrot

½ cup finely diced celery

2¼ cups red wine

2¼ cups Chicken Stock (page 214)

2¼ cups milled tomatoes (see note on page 55)

1 large carrot, peeled and sliced into thin rounds

3 tablespoons roughly chopped tarragon

I have yet to meet an American who didn't like osso buco. A specialty of Milan, every *Nonna* seems to have a recipe for it, and each one will tell you hers is the best. Although veal shanks do take some time to cook, they can be prepared up to four days in advance. Keep them in the fridge and then reheat gently before serving. That way you'll have only the saffron risotto and gremolata to make right before dinner. Gremolata, the combination of finely chopped Italian parsley, lemon, and garlic that is sprinkled over the osso buco after cooking, is the traditional garnish for this dish. For a refreshing variation, use whole parsley leaves and thin strips of lemon zest to create a garnish that resembles a small salad.

NOTE Ask your butcher in advance for portions from the first or second cut of the veal shanks. These pieces have the most meat on them and the bones are filled with marrow. When your butcher realizes you know what you're talking about, he'll be sure to treat you well.

ANOTHER NOTE Because the veal shanks need to be completely covered in liquid while cooking, this recipe creates more sauce than you will probably need for six servings. So do as the Italians do and save the leftover sauce for another day, then reheat it and toss with cooked pasta. Classic pasta shapes for this treatment would be fresh fettuccine, rigatoni, or penne rigate.

Makes 6 entrées

FOR THE OSSO BUCO
- Heat oven to 300°F.
- Tie each veal shank securely with butcher's twine to keep the meat from falling off the bone during cooking.
- Set aside 3 to 5 tablespoons of the flour. Season the veal shanks generously with salt and pepper, dredge in remaining flour, and shake off excess.
- Heat the olive oil in a large sauté pan over high heat on the stovetop.
- When the oil is hot but not smoking, add the veal shanks and sear until golden brown on both sides. Work in batches if needed to avoid overcrowding.
- Remove the veal shanks from the pan and set aside.
- Place butter in the pan and heat to melt.
- Add the garlic, onion, carrot, and celery. Sauté for 2 minutes over high heat.
- Sprinkle 3 tablespoons of reserved flour over the vegetables and stir to incorporate. Add the additional flour if needed, stirring constantly, to make a mixture that resembles very wet sand.
- Add the red wine and cook over high heat for about 3 minutes, stirring and scraping the browned bits from the bottom of the pan with a wooden spoon.
- Transfer the vegetables and sauce to a large roasting pan.

- Stir in the stock and tomatoes, then add the veal shanks, submersing them completely in the liquid.
- Cover the pan with aluminum foil and place in the oven for 3 to 4 hours, checking occasionally to make sure the liquid is very hot, but never boiling.
- To test for doneness, gently pierce the meat with a roasting fork. If it inserts easily and the meat is almost ready to fall from the bone, the shanks are done.
- Remove the pan from the oven and add the sliced carrots and tarragon.
- Let the veal shanks cool slightly, then remove them from the pan. Transfer the cooking liquid and vegetables to a large saucepan and reduce over fairly high heat to a saucelike consistency. (If you are making this in advance, leave the veal shanks in the liquid until the day you are going to serve them, then reheat gently and before reducing the sauce.)

FOR THE SAFFRON RISOTTO
- Bring the chicken stock to a low simmer in a medium sauce pot.
- Heat 1 tablespoon butter and sweat the minced shallot over medium heat in a medium saucepan for 2 minutes, until the shallot is translucent.
- Add the rice to the butter mixture and stir with a wooden spoon for 1 minute.
- Add the saffron and stir for 1 minute.
- Add a pinch of salt and black pepper.
- Add ¾ cup hot chicken stock and continue stirring until most of the liquid has been absorbed.
- Adjust the heat, if needed, to maintain a lively simmer. Continue adding stock in ¾-cup increments, stirring constantly.
- When the rice starts to swell and become tender, begin adding the stock in smaller increments.
- When the rice is al dente and most of the liquid has been absorbed, 18 to 20 minutes, it is finished cooking. The risotto should not be soupy, but creamy and just able to flow out of the pot onto the plate.
- Stir in the remaining butter and the cheese.
- Taste for seasoning and serve.

FOR THE GREMOLATA
- Combine all of the ingredients together in a mixing bowl.
- Do not prepare more than 1 hour in advance.

TO SERVE
- Place a generous spoonful of Saffron Risotto in the center of six large dinner plates.
- Cut and remove the string from the veal shanks, and place one shank on each plate, setting it on top of the risotto.
- Spoon the sauce and the carrots over the veal, garnish with the gremolata, and serve.

FOR THE SAFFRON RISOTTO

4½ cups Chicken Stock (page 214), plus additional if needed

2 tablespoons butter

1 shallot, finely minced

2½ cups Arborio or Carnaroli rice

1 pinch saffron

Salt and pepper

½ cup grated Parmigiano-Reggiano cheese

FOR THE GREMOLATA

½ clove garlic, finely minced

1 heaping tablespoon finely diced lemon zest

1 heaping tablespoon chopped Italian parsley

VEAL MILANESE
WITH ARUGULA, TOMATO, AND RED ONION SALAD

After I made my big move to Boston, I put this on my first menu at Café Louis and people just went crazy for it. The year was 1995, and my guests said I must be a genius or something to have come up with it, where did I get the inspiration? I did not have the heart to tell them that Veal Milanese was on just about every menu in every Italian restaurant in New York City. It is funny how different cities seem to latch onto different dishes. How could something so popular and common in New York be virtually nonexistent in a city just 180 miles north? Ah, let 'em think I made it up. . . .

NOTE This recipe also works well with chicken breast or loin of pork.

Makes 2 lunch or dinner portions

FOR THE VEAL
- Place the flour in a shallow pan and season with salt and pepper.
- Lightly beat the eggs and water in another shallow pan and season with salt and pepper.
- Combine the bread crumbs, thyme, and rosemary in a third shallow pan and season with salt and pepper.
- Arrange the flour, eggwash, and bread crumb pans in a line in front of you, and have a clean platter or pan ready to hold the dredged veal.
- Working with one piece at a time, season the veal with salt and pepper.
- Dip the cutlet in the flour, shaking off any excess, then in the eggwash, allowing the excess egg to drain back into the pan.
- Finally, dip the cutlet in the bread crumbs, pressing gently to coat evenly, and place on the clean platter or pan.
- Refrigerate for at least one hour, or up to six hours.
- Heat the olive oil in a large skillet over high heat. If your pan is not large enough for both pieces of veal, use two pans and divide the olive oil between them.
- When the oil is hot, add the veal and cook about 3 minutes per side, shaking the pan back and forth every 30 seconds or so to create a crisp, golden brown crust.
- Transfer the veal to a plate lined with several layers of paper towels to soak up any excess oil, and season with salt and pepper.

FOR THE SALAD
- Combine the arugula, frisée, tomato, and onion in a mixing bowl.
- Toss the salad with the olive oil, the juice of half the lemon, salt, and pepper.

TO SERVE
- Place the veal in the center of two plates, top with the salad, drizzle with the remaining lemon juice, and serve.

FOR THE VEAL

1 cup flour

Salt and black pepper

2 eggs

2 tablespoons water

1 cup finely ground bread crumbs (preferably panko)

1 pinch fresh thyme leaves, chopped

1 pinch fresh rosemary, chopped

2 5-ounce pieces boneless veal loin, pounded very thin, about ¼-inch thick

4 ounces (½ cup) extra-virgin olive oil

FOR THE SALAD

1 large bunch arugula, rinsed and dried

1 bunch frisée, rinsed and dried (if you cannot find frisée, double the amount of arugula)

1 ripe plum tomato, cut into small dice

½ red onion, thinly sliced

2 ounces (¼ cup) extra-virgin olive oil

Juice of 1 lemon

Salt and pepper, to taste

See next page for how to pound veal (or chicken or steak or pork) into cutlets.

TO POUND VEAL OR CHICKEN OR STEAK OR PORK INTO CUTLETS

Of all the noises in a busy restaurant kitchen, nothing is more certain to drive me up the wall than the sound of meat being pounded into thin cutlets. I always try to have the morning prep crews take care of this task before I get to work so I won't have to listen to the constant *bang-bang-bang* of the mallet smashing meat on the cutting board. But, oh, the results are so worth it.

To be able to enjoy perfect veal or chicken Milanese, or grilled paillards of lamb, venison, or steak, you have to give the meat a good old-fashioned beating to make it tender and thin for quick, even cooking.

Place a slice of meat between two sheets of plastic wrap on the work surface. Using a mallet, pound the meat to an even thickness, about ¼ inch. Go ahead and take your aggressions out, but don't get too rough or the meat will tear. The plastic wrap makes cleanup easier, and the finished product will have a smooth, professional look.

CRUNCHY EGGPLANT

WITH BASIL-MARINATED TOMATOES AND
SHAVED PARMIGIANO-REGGIANO

This version of *eggplant alla Parmigiana* is without question the most popular item on the menu at Via Matta. I first tasted it while traveling in the hills of Chianti, where I stayed at Castello di Monsanto. One afternoon I had the good fortune of eating with the owners of the Monsanto winery, the Bianchi family. They were incredibly hospitable (as most Italians are) and wanted to show off with an amazing meal. It was so simply prepared, yet it paired beautifully with their world-class wines.

The Bianchis invited me to select a bottle of their superb Il Poggio for the meal, and during the tour of their wine cave I learned about a brilliant family custom: Whenever someone in the immediate family has a baby, cases and cases of that year's wine are put away. The wine is placed in a special section of the cave with the baby's name overhead. It remains there untouched until the child's wedding day, when it is served at the reception.

Any of us could start a similar tradition. Even storing a single bottle from the birth year of the child, to be shared by close family members on the wedding day, would be a very thoughtful custom.

TRUC To shave Parmigiano-Reggiano cheese, use a sharp knife to cut the flat side of a wedge of cheese as thinly as possible into long sheets. If you have trouble with this, use a vegetable peeler. The sheets won't be as big, but the effect will be similar.

NOTE You can prepare the tomatoes up to six hours in advance. Any longer than that, and they begin to break down from the salt. Likewise, the eggplant can be breaded several hours in advance and refrigerated.

Makes 4 first courses

- Place the flour in a shallow pan and season with salt and pepper.
- Beat the eggs and water in another shallow pan and season with salt and pepper.
- Combine the bread crumbs, thyme, and rosemary in a third shallow pan and season with salt and pepper
- Season the eggplant slices with salt and pepper.
- Dip an eggplant slice in the flour, shaking off any excess, then in the egg-wash, allowing the excess egg to drain back into the pan, then in the bread crumbs, pressing gently to coat evenly. Place on a clean platter or pan and repeat with the remaining slices.

directions are continued on following page

---

1 cup flour

Salt and pepper

2 eggs

2 tablespoons water

1 cup bread crumbs (preferably panko)

1 pinch fresh thyme, chopped

1 pinch fresh rosemary, chopped

4 2-inch-thick eggplant rounds, unpeeled (select the largest eggplant you can find)

6 ounces (¾ cup) extra-virgin olive oil

4 heaping tablespoons Basil-Marinated Tomatoes (recipe follows)

8 to 12 "sheets" shaved Parmigiano-Reggiano cheese

- Refrigerate for at least 30 minutes.
- Preheat the oven to 500°F.
- Remove the eggplant from the fridge 10 minutes before cooking.
- Heat the olive oil in a large sauté pan over high heat for 2 minutes.
- Add the eggplant slices, being careful not to crowd them. (cook in two batches if your pan is small).
- Fry the eggplant until golden brown on both sides, 2 to 3 minutes per side.
- Transfer the eggplant to a baking sheet and place in the hot oven for 15 minutes.
- Remove from the oven and pat with paper towel to remove any excess oil.
- Place each slice on a plate, top with the Basil-Marinated Tomatoes, garnish generously with the shaved Parmigiano, and serve.

BASIL-MARINATED TOMATOES

Makes 1½ cups

4 ripe plum tomatoes, cut into medium dice

8 to 10 large basil leaves, torn into small pieces

2 ounces (¼ cup) really good quality extra-virgin olive oil

Juice of half a lemon

Salt, pepper, and crushed red pepper

This is incredibly versatile stuff, delicious hot or cold. In addition to this eggplant dish, you can use it to top bruschetta, grilled fish or vegetables, or toss it with pasta.

- Combine everything in a bowl and let marinate for at least two hours.
- Before serving, drain some of the liquid, or else use a slotted spoon to serve.

PANNA COTTA
WITH APRICOT CONFIT

This version of the classic Italian dessert was created by PJ Waters, the pastry chef at Via Matta. PJ is constantly researching old Italian recipes, updating them, and giving them beautiful presentations, yet he always pays respect to the originals, so his interpretations remain very "Italian."

Makes 6 desserts

FOR THE APRICOT CONFIT
- Blanch the apricots in salted boiling water for 2 minutes.
- Drain apricots and shock in a bowl of ice water.
- Peel the skins from the apricots and remove pits.
- Combine apricots and sugar in a saucepot and simmer over low heat until the fruit breaks up slightly, 5 to 7 minutes. You can stop now, or if a smooth confit is desired, transfer to the bowl of a food processor and pulse to a coarse puree.
- Refrigerate until well chilled.

FOR THE PANNA COTTA
- Sprinkle gelatin over cold water in a small bowl and let stand 5 minutes, until dissolved.
- Warm cream, sugar, salt, vanilla extract, and vanilla bean in a medium saucepan over medium heat.
- Remove from heat, stir in gelatin mixture, and let cool for 10 to 15 minutes.
- Remove the vanilla bean
- Whisk in the sour cream.

TO SERVE
- Line up six tall, clear glasses. Spoon about 1½ ounces (3 tablespoons) confit into each glass.
- Divide the panna cotta between the glasses and chill for 1 hour.
- Spoon more apricot confit on top of the panna cotta, cover with plastic wrap, and return to the refrigerator. (It can be stored for up to two days.)
- Just before serving, garnish each panna cotta with a tablespoon of crushed pistachios.

FOR THE
APRICOT CONFIT

6 ripe apricots

½ cup sugar

FOR THE
PANNA COTTA

2½ teaspoons gelatin

2 tablespoons cold water

3 cups heavy cream

½ cup sugar

1 pinch salt

1½ teaspoons vanilla extract

½ vanilla bean

1 cup sour cream

6 tablespoons crushed pistachios for garnish

ALMOND BISCOTTI

4 cups all-purpose flour

⅔ cup sugar

½ teaspoon salt

1¼ teaspoons baking powder

2 teaspoons aniseed

Zest of 1 lemon, grated

Zest of 1 lime, grated

Zest of 1 orange, grated

4 whole eggs

4 egg yolks

1¼ teaspoons vanilla

2 cups whole almonds

The classic ending to an Italian meal. Dip these into a glass of *vin santo* (Tuscan dessert wine) until they soften just enough so you won't risk breaking a tooth.

Makes about 40 biscotti

- Preheat the oven to 325°F.
- Combine the flour, sugar, salt, baking powder, aniseed, lemon zest, lime zest, and orange zest in a mixing bowl.
- In another mixing bowl, whisk together the eggs, yolks, and vanilla until thick and light in color.
- Add the beaten eggs to the flour mixture and stir to combine.
- Add the almonds and stir until the dough comes together.
- Divide the dough into two pieces and roll into logs, 2 inches in diameter. Lightly flour the work surface if needed to keep the dough from sticking.
- Transfer the logs to baking sheets lined with parchment paper, placing them at least 4 inches apart so they do not stick to each other during baking.
- Bake for about 30 minutes, until golden.
- Allow to cool for 30 minutes.
- Cut the logs on a slight bias into 1-inch-thick slices. Return the slices to the baking sheet and bake in the oven for 20 to 30 minutes, until the biscotti are dry and hard.
- Let cool, then store in an airtight container.

Chapter 4

TIME FOR THE ULTIMATE SUMMER BBQ

ORGANIZING AND ENJOYING YOUR PARTY

In Boston, the winters are eight weeks too long. By the time summer comes, we're like crazed little puppies racing to get outside. And when you finally do get to throw on some shorts and feel the sun on your face, what's on the social calendar? The dreaded bad barbecue. You've been to them, yes, all of you have. Could you possibly be the culprit who throws them once in a while? The hamburgers are overcooked, the buns are burnt, the hot dogs — well, they really aren't even hot dogs, they're more in the wiener family and we all know that is a whole other category. Pounds of store-made potato salad, coleslaw, and macaroni salad baking in the sun. Yes Virginia, the supermarkets sure have made it easy on all of us! Well, look at the bright side — at least we're outside.

I'm not trying to be a food snob here. I love barbecues — really I do. I don't want to get rid of them altogether. I just want to improve them a bit. My ideas and recipes will help you throw a truly great barbecue; you and your guests will still be able to experience the nostalgia we all associate with grilling outside and that we all crave when the weather is warm.

Wouldn't a barbecue be better with a truly great hamburger? You know you want one, but you've been let down so many times in the past that your expectations are pretty low. With my Schlow Burger (trademark pending), not only will you get a great hamburger, you'll add dimension with a delicious and easy horseradish sauce. Want to make it a cheeseburger? Great. But top it with some aged sharp English or Vermont cheddar instead of those pre-wrapped slices. There is no need to buy barbecue sauce for the ribs; it's easy enough to make, and you can prepare it days in advance. You can customize it as you like, and you'll be that much prouder when someone asks, "Where did you get that terrific barbecue sauce?" Of course, there's such a thing as going overboard. Making your own ketchup? I actually think Heinz is pretty close to perfection.

When hosting a barbecue, it's important to work with the weather, not against it. On a sweltering day, a granita would certainly be a refreshing dessert, but don't bring it to the picnic table in a big bowl — it'll melt in seconds. Instead, prepare the ice in advance, place it in individual glasses, and have it waiting in the freezer. When it's time for dessert, bring the glasses out on a tray, and your guests can grab their own. They will love you for this.

When cooking for a crowd, make it easy on yourself and do as much as possible ahead of time. I remember a summer barbecue I threw for 70 staff members in my backyard. My goal was to stay outside with my guests, so I got as much done in advance as possible. I arranged a big buffet at the beginning of the party. (I love the look of a lot of food out on a large wooden table for an event like this.) Then all I had to do was tend the grill and fork over the hot goods to my guests. I made a point to serve foods that are equally good hot or at room temperature; dishes like grilled chicken, for instance, that can be enjoyed straight from the grill or allowed to cool slowly.

Think of this chapter as a set menu, but with interchangeable parts. Whether you want to make two of these dishes or ten, go ahead, knock yourself out. I've tried to strike a balance between the tried and true and recipes that offer an unexpected twist here and there. Like the potato salad — I've spiced it up with a little chipotle pepper to give it some smokiness and heat. And instead of making a three-bean salad with beans from a can, I'm providing a recipe for a beautiful string bean salad with sliced red onion and prosciutto.

Since no barbecue is complete without ice-cold beverages, I've included recipes for mixed and blended drinks that will cure your thirst and then some. And you can't forget the metal washtub filled with ice, beer, soda, and tequila — the bottles with that icy condensation on them, you reach in, your hand gets so cold finding your favorite . . . it's finally summertime!

THE SCHLOW BURGER

WITH CHEDDAR, CRISPY ONIONS, AND HORSERADISH SAUCE

18 ounces ground beef (Ask the butcher for 80 percent lean. Do not change this part, please!)

1 ounce (2 tablespoons) extra-virgin olive oil

Salt and pepper

4 tablespoons mayonnaise

2 teaspoons prepared white horseradish

Juice of half a lemon

2 thick slices good quality Vermont or English cheddar cheese

2 hamburger buns, split in half (buy the best ones you can get; I like brioche buns)

Crispy Onions (recipe follows)

Fresh ground pepper

I really never thought I would be writing down this recipe, but everyone with an opinion and a say-so said, "You gotta put it in the book." So here goes — try this burger once and see if it doesn't make you change the way you order your burgers. Someday, maybe I'll open a burger joint and feature this colossal, monster of a sandwich on the menu, but for now I'll stick to making it in my own backyard.

NOTE The sauce can be made up to three days ahead; the onions can be prepared early on the day they will be served.

Makes 2 "fat boy" burgers

- Combine the ground beef with the olive oil, salt, and plenty of black pepper.
- Divide the meat into two 9-ounce patties and refrigerate until the grill is ready. (Don't do this more than an hour in advance.)
- Combine mayonnaise, horseradish, and lemon juice in a mixing bowl and season with black pepper. (You can do this ahead of time and store it in the fridge.)
- Heat the grill to high.
- Take the hamburgers out of the refrigerator 5 to 7 minutes before you are ready to grill them.
- Place the burgers on the preheated grill and cook 1½ minutes (for rare).
- Give the burgers a quarter-turn to "mark" them, and cook 1½ more minutes.
- Flip the burgers over and cook 1½ minutes.
- Rotate a quarter-turn to "mark" and cook 1½ more minutes.
- Transfer the burgers to the grill's top shelf or to a cooler section of the grill and cover each one with a slice of cheese.
- Turn the grill off and shut the lid.
- After 4 minutes, open the lid. The cheese will be melted and the burgers cooked rare to medium-rare. Toast the buns, if desired, and place a burger on each.
- Spread plenty of the horseradish sauce on each burger; it should drip down the sides.
- Top with Crispy Onions and season with freshly ground black pepper.
- Slather more sauce on the other half of the bun and place it on top of the burger.
- Grab a cold beer or iced tea and get ready to make a mess. This is not a dainty meal!

CRISPY ONIONS

1 large yellow onion, sliced into very thin rings, ⅓- to ⅛-inch thick

2 cups canola oil

You might think onions would need to be coated in flour before frying to make them crispy, but that's not necessarily true. Here's a little method (patent pending) that gives you not only crunchy onions, but onions that will stay that way for quite a while, even overnight, if stored in an airtight container lined with paper towels. It works great with shallots, too.

Makes about ½ cup, enough for 2 Schlow Burgers

- Place onion rings and oil in a small sauce pot. (Don't worry if the rings break apart; it won't ruin the final product.)
- Bring to a boil over high heat, and then reduce heat to a very low simmer. The heat releases the onion's natural sugars, and in essence, causes them to melt.
- Turn the onions with a fork every thirty seconds or so, and cook until they turn golden brown, 12 to 15 minutes. Adjust the heat if needed to maintain a low simmer.
- Remove the onions from the oil and arrange in a single layer on paper towels. (At this point the onions won't yet be crispy, but I promise you that after a few minutes, as the caramelized sugars cool and harden, the onions will become deliciously crisp.)

CRUNCHY STRING BEAN SALAD
WITH RED ONION AND PROSCIUTTO

3 pounds fresh string beans, ends snipped

3 tablespoons salt

1 to 2 small red onions, thinly sliced (about 2 cups)

10 to 12 thin slices prosciutto di Parma, julienned

6 ounces (¾ cup) extra-virgin olive oil

Juice of 2 lemons

1 tablespoon chopped fresh rosemary

Salt, pepper, and crushed red pepper flakes

At summer barbecues, I serve this salad chilled. Heated, it makes a great accompaniment to roasted or grilled meats. Lamb, steak, chicken, roast pork — it goes well with them all.

NOTE The beans can be cooked a day in advance, if you like.

Makes a big bowl, enough for a small crowd

- Bring a large pot of water to a boil and add the salt.
- Fill a large bowl with ice water and set it beside the sink.
- Blanch the string beans in the salted water for 1 to 2 minutes, until cooked but still slightly crunchy, then strain and plunge in ice water for 2 minutes.
- Strain beans, transfer to a bowl, and refrigerate. (The beans can stay in the fridge for up to a day.)
- Remove beans from the fridge 1 hour before serving. Add the onions and prosciutto. (This can either be done in advance or when you dress the salad.)
- Just before bringing the salad to the table, mix in the oil, lemon juice, rosemary, salt, pepper, and crushed red pepper flakes.
- Taste for seasoning, add more oil or lemon if necessary, and serve.

GRILLED CHICKEN
WITH AVOCADO, GREEN CHILE, AND TOMATO SALSA

Which green chile to use is up to you — it all depends on how spicy you like your salsa. Want it mild? Use a poblano or New Mexican green chile. More picante? Try a jalapeño. And if you're really tough, go for a scotch bonnet or habanero!

NOTE Any leftovers make for great sandwiches the next day.

TRUC To dice an avocado, cut it in half lengthwise with a sharp knife. Remove the pit but do not peel yet. Score vertical and horizontal slices in the meat of the avocado to make a grid. Squeeze lime juice over the exposed surface, and then push the meat out and away from the skin using your fingers or a spoon. Squeeze more lime juice on the avocado to prevent discoloring.

Makes a platter for 8

- Turn the grill to high.
- Place the diced avocado in a mixing bowl and drizzle with the juice of 1 lime to prevent browning.
- Add the chile, tomatoes, red onion, 1 tablespoon of cilantro, a small pinch of cayenne pepper, cumin, and 2 tablespoons of olive oil. Season with salt and pepper.
- Fold the ingredients together gently so as not to break up the avocado too much. Taste and adjust the seasoning, if needed.
- Season the chicken with salt, pepper, a small pinch of cayenne pepper, and 1 tablespoon cilantro. Drizzle the remaining olive oil over the chicken.
- Place the chicken on the preheated grill and cook 1½ minutes.
- Give the chicken breasts a quarter-turn to "mark" them, and cook 1½ more minutes.
- Flip the chicken over and cook 1½ minutes.
- Rotate a quarter-turn to "mark" and cook 1½ more minutes.
- Move to the top shelf or the coolest part of the grill and close the lid. Turn the heat off.
- Cook for 5 minutes more, or until done.
- Transfer chicken breasts to a platter, top with salsa, and garnish with cilantro sprigs.
- Squeeze the remaining lime over the top and serve.

4 ripe avocados, halved, pitted, and cut into medium dice

Juice of 2 limes

1 roasted green chile, peeled, seeded, and chopped

3 plum tomatoes, cut into small dice

½ red onion, finely diced

2 tablespoons chopped fresh cilantro

Cayenne pepper, to taste

1 pinch ground cumin

4 ounces (8 tablespoons) extra-virgin olive oil (2 tablespoons for the salsa, and the rest for drizzling on the chicken before grilling)

Salt and pepper

8 large boneless, skinless chicken breast halves

5 cilantro sprigs, for garnish

See next page for how to roast chiles & other peppers

TO ROAST CHILES AND OTHER PEPPERS This simple method will ensure you get the most flavor possible out of roasted peppers: Grill chiles over an open flame (use your grill, or place the chiles over a gas burner or under the broiler). Turn the chiles as they cook, allowing them to char on all sides. When they are blackened all over, place in a mixing bowl and cover tightly with plastic wrap. When the chiles are cool enough to handle, remove all the blistered and blackened skin with your fingers or a paring knife. Do not rinse under water, as this will wash away all their smoky flavor. Since most of a chile's heat comes from the seeds, remove or leave them, as you like. The more seeds, the hotter the final dish.

WITHOUT QUESTION eggs are one of the hardest items to cook perfectly. I am forever in awe of talented short-order cooks who field rapid-fire strings of breakfast tickets in a busy diner. But the thought of poaching eggs needn't stop you in your tracks. Here's how: Fill a small sauce pot three-quarters full with water. Bring it to a boil, add 2 capfuls of white vinegar, and lower the heat to a simmer. Carefully crack the eggs directly into the water and simmer for 3 minutes for soft-poached. Remove the eggs with a slotted spoon to drain the excess water and serve.

CREAMY POTATO SALAD

WITH CHIPOTLE PEPPERS AND GREEN ONION

Although this creamy potato salad can be served warm or cold, make sure it is well-chilled for a summer barbecue. Trust me, when everyone is coated with sunblock and overheated from playing horseshoes, no one wants hot potato salad. I speak from experience; I tried it one scorching August day. Not a big hit.

TRUC *Lardons* are delicious little pieces of smoked bacon, cut thicker than your average store-bought bacon. To make them, buy slab bacon and cut it yourself into ¼-inch-thick slices, then cut the slices into ½-inch pieces. Put the slices in a sauté pan over high heat without any additional oil or liquid. Once the bacon starts to render, turn the heat to low and begin pouring the fat off. Continue rendering and pouring off the fat for 10 to 15 minutes, until the bacon is almost cooked, then add 2 tablespoons water to the pan. Simmer, adding more water if it boils away before the bacon is fully cooked. When the bacon is evenly browned, raise the heat to medium-high and allow any remaining water to reduce until it has all evaporated.

Makes 8 to 12 side dishes

- Boil the potatoes in plenty of salted water roughly 20 minutes, or until tender.
- Meanwhile, softly poach the eggs (see sidebar on page 92) until the whites are firm but the yolks are still fairly runny, about 3 minutes. Remove with a slotted spoon and set aside.
- Drain the potatoes and combine while still hot with the eggs, chipotle pepper, adobo sauce, scallions, red onion, bacon, carrot, olive oil, and vinegar. (The eggs will break up on their own as the salad is tossed.)
- Cool for 10 to 15 minutes, then stir in the mayonnaise. (The salad can be prepared to this point a couple of hours ahead of serving.)
- Right before serving, add the parsley, salt, and pepper, and mix well. Taste and adjust the seasoning. If the salad seems dry, add a bit more oil, mayonnaise, or vinegar, depending on your taste. Serve.

3 pounds red bliss potatoes, quartered

3 eggs

1 chipotle pepper, seeds removed and very finely chopped (see page 101 for a tip on buying chipotle peppers)

1 teaspoon adobo sauce

1 cup sliced scallions, green and white parts

½ red onion, thinly sliced

2 thick slices bacon, rendered into crisp lardons

1 carrot, quartered lengthwise, then thinly sliced

3 ounces (6 tablespoons) extra-virgin olive oil

1 ounce (2 tablespoons) sherry vinegar

3 tablespoons mayonnaise

3 tablespoons roughly chopped Italian parsley

Salt and pepper

BACKYARD SPECIAL
LOBSTER BAKE FOR 2

6 ounces (¾ cup) extra-virgin olive oil

4 ounces (½ cup) water

1 sprig fresh rosemary

1 sprig fresh thyme

2 tablespoons Old Bay Seasoning

½ white onion, thinly sliced

4 lemons, halved

2 1½ pound live lobsters

12 jumbo shrimp, shells on

24 steamer clams (see page 62 for a tip on cleaning clams)

6 red bliss potatoes, quartered and blanched until tender, then plunged in ice water to prevent overcooking

2 ears corn, husked and rubbed to remove any silk

Salt and pepper

WARNING *This might not be first-date material. Instead it's a meal meant to be shared by two people who know each other well and don't mind sitting in silence while making an absolute mess in front of one another.*

Okay, I admit it, in my backyard I have one of those fancy grills with the burners on the side; in fact, I think my brother, Robert, suffers from grill envy whenever he watches me use it. If you happen to have one too, bring it into service for this dinner. If your grill gets hot enough to keep a stockpot at a boil, you can cook this "cowboy style" with the pot sitting directly on the grill. If space is an issue, grill the corn first, then return the ears to the grill to reheat during the last few minutes of cooking.

Definitely not as much fun, but still equally effective, you can cook the lobsters indoors on the stove.

- Turn on the grill to high.
- Put 2 ounces (4 tablespoons) olive oil, water, rosemary, thyme, 1 tablespoon of the Old Bay Seasoning, and onion in a large, deep stockpot and set over high heat on the grill's burner, or directly on the grill. (If your grill doesn't have a separate burner and the stock won't reach a rolling boil on the grill itself, you're probably better off doing this indoors over the stove.)
- Squeeze the juice of two lemons into the pot, then throw the lemon halves in too.
- Cook, covered, for 3 minutes.
- Meanwhile, rub the corn with 2 ounces (4 tablespoons) olive oil, salt, and black pepper. Place on the top shelf of the grill and close the lid.
- Add the lobster to the boiling stockpot and cook, covered, for 4 minutes.
- Begin turning the corn to brown on all sides. Lower the heat if it is cooking too quickly.
- Sprinkle the shrimp with the remaining Old Bay Seasoning and add to the lobster pot.
- Cover and cook for 1 minute.
- Add the clams and cover again. Cook for 1 minute.
- Season the cooked potatoes with salt and pepper and throw them into the lobster pot.
- Cover, and when the clams open, the dish is done.

TO SERVE
- Remove the contents of the lobster pot and arrange them in a shallow serving dish.
- Drizzle the remaining olive oil on the corn, sprinkle with salt, and add to the lobster dish.
- Strain the cooking broth from the pot into a small bowl, and bring to the table for dipping the steamer clams.
- Garnish the serving dish with the remaining lemon halves.
- Grab a bowl for the shells, stop talking, and start eating!

GRILLED VEGETABLES
THAT MAKE SENSE

Grilling vegetables can be a humbling experience for even the most expert barbecuer. Who hasn't lost a couple of onion slices through the racks? Or tried to grill something that really should not be grilled, like Brussels sprouts' leaves?

The most frequent complaint I hear is, "How come I can never get the vegetables and meat to finish grilling at the same time?" Well, the trick is all in the timing, and knowing how thick or thin to cut the vegetables so everything tastes great and comes off the grill together.

NOTE Garnish the grilled vegetables with a few spoonfuls of Basil-Marinated Tomatoes (page 76), and they easily become a summer meal on their own.

TRUC Asparagus almost talks to you, revealing where the tender eating stops and the tough, stringy part begins (usually where the green color starts to turn white). Just bend the spear gently toward you at about its lower third, and it will snap where the good and bad should part ways.

ANOTHER TRUC Pour a couple ounces of canola oil on a clean rag and rub it on the preheated grill racks to keep vegetables from sticking.

Makes dinner for 2 or side dishes for 4

- Turn your grill to high, make sure it is brushed clean, and rub it with canola oil to keep the vegetables from sticking.
- Whisk the olive oil, vinegar, herbs, a large pinch of salt, a few grindings of black pepper, and a pinch of crushed red pepper flakes in a small bowl.
- Put the peppers on the grill for 2 minutes, then follow with the rest of the vegetables. To prevent the asparagus from falling through the cracks, lay them crosswise on the grill.
- Lower the heat to medium so the vegetables do not burn.
- Lightly brush each vegetable with the olive oil and herb mixture and grill 3 to 4 minutes.
- Turn the vegetables over and continue basting. (Be careful not to burn anything; the oil will cause the flames to flare up.)
- If any one vegetable is intent on going up in flames or it is blackening or cooking much faster than the others, transfer it to the top rack or a cooler section of your grill and let the other vegetables catch up.
- All of the vegetables should take roughly 6 to 8 minutes to become tender. The endive and radicchio should be just lightly charred; remove them to the shelf or a cooler section of the grill to prevent overcooking, if needed.
- Transfer vegetables to a serving platter or individual plates and season with salt and pepper.
- Drizzle any of the remaining oil and herb mixture over the top, give it all a squeeze of lemon, and serve.

FOR THE
BASTING MIXTURE

4 ounces (½ cup) extra-virgin olive oil

2 ounces (¼ cup) sherry vinegar

1 large pinch fresh rosemary, chopped

1 large pinch fresh thyme leaves, chopped

1 large pinch fresh tarragon, chopped

Salt, pepper, and crushed red pepper flakes

FOR THE
VEGETABLES

1 red pepper, quartered lengthwise, pith and seeds removed

1 yellow pepper, quartered lengthwise, pith and seeds removed

1 medium zucchini, cut on a slight bias, ¾-inch thick

1 medium yellow squash, cut on a slight bias, ¾-inch thick

12 asparagus spears, trimmed

1 head endive, halved lengthwise

1 head radicchio, halved

1 lemon, halved

THE BEST FLANK STEAK

1 large flank steak
(1½ to 2 pounds)

Salt and pepper, for
seasoning the steak
before grilling

FOR THE MARINADE

4 ounces (½ cup) extra-virgin
olive oil

2 ounces (¼ cup) sherry vinegar

1 ounce (2 tablespoons)
balsamic vinegar

2 ounces (¼ cup) water

1 tablespoon ketchup

½ teaspoon
Worcestershire sauce

1 teaspoon honey

1 teaspoon sugar

½ red onion, very finely diced

1 pinch cayenne pepper

1 teaspoon chopped
fresh rosemary

½ teaspoon chopped fresh
thyme leaves

½ teaspoon pepper

Well, that is a rather bold statement, don't you think? I don't really know if this is the best flank steak ever, but it certainly is the best one I've ever tasted. It is the one I grew up with, and if you serve it with Grilled Vegetables That Make Sense (page 97), I think you have a near-perfect summer meal.

If there is any flank steak left over, dice it up the following morning and add to some crispy sautéed potatoes, onions, and peppers. Top with scrambled or soft-poached eggs, then mix everything together and add a little hot sauce and cracked black pepper. You'll have a steak-and-egg breakfast like you've never even dreamed about.

NOTE A prolonged stint in the marinade helps develop the rich flavor of this steak, so let it marinate a full 24 hours; 36 is even better.

TRUC Be sure to slice the meat across the grain. If you look at the steak, you will see little "ridges" that run from one side of the meat to the other. Simply slice across these ridges (rather than along them) on a slight bias and you will notice a huge difference in the texture of the final dish. The meat will be much more tender and easy to chew; slicing with the grain results in tough, stringy meat.

Makes 4 portions

TO MARINATE THE STEAK

- At least 24 hours before serving, place all ingredients except steak in a mixing bowl and whisk well to combine.
- Put the flank steak in a large, ziplock bag and add the marinade mixture.
- Seal the bag and refrigerate 24 to 36 hours.

TO GRILL

- Thirty minutes before grilling, remove the steak from the fridge. Transfer it to a platter and reserve the marinade for basting.
- Preheat your grill to high
- Season the steak with salt and pepper.
- Place the steak on the hot grill and cook 1 to 2 minutes.
- Rotate the steak a quarter-turn to mark the steak, which promotes even cooking and makes an attractive grill pattern on the meat.
- Cook for 1 to 2 minutes more, then flip to sear the other side. Dab the marinade onto the meat with a pastry brush.
- Cook for 1 to 2 minutes, then mark by rotating a quarter-turn.
- Cook for another 1 to 2 minutes and continue to baste.
- Reduce the heat to low and transfer the steak to the warming shelf placed

in the highest position. If you don't have a warming shelf, move the meat to a cooler section of the grill.

- Close the lid and continue cooking 8 to 12 more minutes for medium-rare, depending on the thickness of the meat. Lift the lid to turn the steak over and baste with the marinade every 2 minutes or so.
- Allow the meat to rest for 5 minutes off to the side of the grill.
- Cut steak across the grain on a slight bias into thin slices (¼- to ⅛-inch thick) and serve.

COUSIN SHARI'S COLESLAW

My cousin Shari's coleslaw is famous at our family barbecues. The recipe is actually from her mother, my aunt Eleanor, and I have to admit to devouring copious quantities of it at a sitting — whatever the occasion. It is simple to prepare and delicious. Barbecues have a way of making people feel nostalgic, and we certainly do get nostalgic about my aunt when we eat this.

Makes 4 to 6 side dishes

- Combine the onion and sugar in a large mixing bowl and let sit for 30 minutes.
- Add the olive oil, vinegar, mayonnaise, salt, and pepper and stir well to combine.
- Fifteen to 30 minutes before serving, add the cabbage, toss well, and refrigerate until serving time.

1 medium yellow onion, chopped into small dice

1 cup sugar

8 ounces (1 cup) pure or extra-virgin olive oil

4 ounces (½ cup) apple cider vinegar

⅔ cup mayonnaise

1 teaspoon salt

½ teaspoon pepper

1 large head green cabbage, shredded

COUNTRY RIBS
WITH HOMEMADE BARBECUE SAUCE

It is always a toss-up: pork or beef ribs at a barbecue? Personally, I can never refuse good barbecued anything. I love it all! Since most people do not own a smoker, I have devised a recipe that will give you the most tender ribs possible without one. They are easy to prepare, and most of the work can be done days in advance. Ask your butcher to save you the best, meatiest ribs from racks of large pork or beef rib-eyes, and search the international or specialty foods section of your supermarket for a can of chipotle peppers in adobo sauce. Chipotle peppers are smoked, dried jalapeños, and they will unlock the secret to great, homemade barbecued foods. If used sparingly, they impart fantastic background notes of smokiness and spice.

NOTE The sauce can also be used on chicken, pork loin, or grilled brisket.
ANOTHER NOTE If you are having a "mega-BBQ" for a hundred people I would not suggest this dish. It works better for parties with 15 or fewer guests.

For 6 orders (2 ribs apiece)

FOR THE RIBS
- The first step, cooking the ribs, needs to happen at least one day before the barbecue. To begin, season the ribs generously with salt and pepper.
- Preheat the oven to 250°F.
- Place the ribs in a roasting pan deep enough to hold them all, and add just enough canola oil to cover them completely.
- Bake slowly for 3 to 4 hours, checking periodically to make sure the oil is hot but not boiling. Adjust heat if needed.
- When the meat starts to pull away, leaving a clean bone at the bottom of the rib, remove the pan from the oven and allow to cool completely.
- Cover the pan with foil and put the whole works in the fridge. The ribs will keep for several days, as long as the oil is completely covering them.
- On the day of the barbecue, an hour before serving, take the pan out of the fridge and place in a 225°F oven for 10 minutes to make the ribs easier to remove from the oil. Transfer the ribs to a colander set over a platter and drain off any excess oil.

FOR THE SAUCE (which can be made several days in advance)
- Combine all of the sauce ingredients in a bowl and mix well.
- Adjust the seasoning, adding more spices, more honey, or more vinegar to suit your taste.

TO GRILL
- Heat the grill to medium-high.

directions are continued on following page

FOR THE RIBS

12 large, meaty country ribs, bone-in (beef or pork)

Salt and pepper

Canola oil (you are going to need a lot; buy a gallon — it keeps)

FOR THE SAUCE

2 cups ketchup

2 tablespoons orange marmalade

1 tablespoon brown sugar

2 heaping tablespoons adobo sauce (from a can of chipotle peppers in adobo sauce; save the actual pepper for Creamy Potato Salad, page 93)

1 pinch ground cumin

2 tablespoons honey

½ teaspoon Worcestershire sauce

1 tablespoon balsamic vinegar

1 tablespoon Dijon mustard

1 tablespoon salt

¼ teaspoon cayenne

2 ounces (¼ cup) orange juice

- Season the ribs with additional salt and pepper and place on the grill.
- Grill the ribs for 2 minutes per side, then start basting them with the sauce.
- Cook for another 5 to 7 minutes, turning and basting every 2 minutes.
- Reduce the heat if the ribs start to blacken too much. (Because of the high sugar content, they are supposed to burn a little.) When the sauce adheres to the ribs and begins to caramelize, the ribs are done.
- Coat the ribs one last time with the sauce and serve.

SLOW-GRILLED PORK
WITH HERB RUB

FOR THE GRILLED PORK

6 8-ounce slices center-cut boneless pork loin (1½-inches thick)

Salt and pepper

FOR THE HERB RUB

1 heaping teaspoon chopped fresh rosemary

1 heaping teaspoon chopped fresh thyme leaves

1 heaping teaspoon chopped fresh tarragon

1 heaping teaspoon chopped fresh mint

1 heaping teaspoon chopped fresh Italian parsley

2 tablespoons finely minced shallots

2 ounces (4 tablespoons) orange juice

2 ounces (4 tablespoons) extra-virgin olive oil

Salt, pepper, and cayenne pepper

You don't have to throw a barbecue to enjoy this pork loin. I make it year-round — I've even been known to go outside and brush the snow off the grill in January just to prepare it. By now you might have noticed I am not in favor of cooking things at high, intense heat. Although I like to get the grill good and hot to start, I lower the heat once the actual cooking begins, and I sometimes even move the food to higher ground on the top racks to protect it from the direct flames. The results, I've found, are more juicy and flavorful, and this pork loin is no exception.

Makes 6 servings

- Turn the grill to high.
- Combine the ingredients for the herb rub in a small bowl. The paste will be slightly moist.
- Season the pork with salt and pepper.
- Rub the herb mixture liberally on all sides of the pork chops; there should not be any left.
- Place the pork on the grill, reduce the heat to medium, and close the lid.
- Sear 1 to 2 minutes, then give the pork a quarter-turn to mark it.
- Close the lid again and cook 2 more minutes.
- Flip the pork over to sear the other side, close the lid, and cook 2 minutes.
- Rotate the pork a quarter-turn to mark again. Close the lid and continue to cook another 2 minutes.
- Transfer the pork to the highest rack or a cooler section of the grill, close the lid, and let meat finish cooking, about 5 more minutes.
- Serve.

LATTE GRANITA

You don't need a summer barbecue as an excuse to serve this granita. Keep it in your freezer and save it for any occasion requiring a dessert that is slightly sweet and not too heavy. Softly whipped cream flavored with a touch of cinnamon really tops it off.

4 cups strong coffee, cooled

2 cups whole milk

1 cup sugar

Makes 6 to 8 servings

- Combine all of the ingredients in a large mixing bowl and whisk until the sugar is dissolved.
- Transfer the coffee mixture to a deep glass baking dish or stainless steel pan.
- Place in the freezer for 30 minutes.
- Stir the mixture well to break up the ice crystals forming around the edge of the dish.
- Return to the freezer and continue stirring every 30 minutes until the granita has frozen into light, flakey crystals, about 2 hours. You can store the granita in the freezer for some time, but you may need to reflake with a fork.
- On the day you are going to serve the granita, spoon it into chilled glasses and place in the freezer. Garnish with whipped cream just before serving, if desired.

SPECIALTY DRINKS OF THE HOUSE Every outdoor event needs ice-cold beverages, and these specialty drinks will certainly prove refreshing. Not only will they keep your party lively, they will extend your repertoire well beyond the average margarita or gin and tonic.

NOTE To make simple syrup, which is required for many of these drinks, bring 1 cup sugar and 1 cup water to a boil in a small sauce pot. Boil until the sugar is completely dissolved, then transfer to a plastic container and refrigerate until needed. Keeps for at least a week.

JIMMY'S DANCING PUNCH

4 ounces good-quality vodka

4 ounces good-quality gin

4 ounces good-quality white rum

4 ounces good-quality tequila

4 ounces good-quality champagne or prosecco

8 ounces orange juice

8 ounces pineapple juice

1 pint strawberry sorbet or ice cream

2 cups ice

Fresh strawberries or orange slices, for garnish

Jimmy P. is a good friend of mine and a regular at Via Matta. After finishing his meal, he often decides it's time to be our guest bartender. He makes himself at home behind the bar, and when he mixes up this crazy concoction, the guests who consume it usually end up dancing around the room, which is how this potent libation got its name.

Makes 1 quart punch

- Place everything in either a large shaker or blender and mix well.
- Serve with more ice and garnish with fresh strawberries or orange slices.

BLACKBERRY SAGE ITALIAN SODA

4 fresh blackberries

3 fresh whole sage leaves

¼ ounce simple syrup

Ice

2 ounces citron vodka

Splash amaretto

Splash cassis

Splash orange juice

Splash soda water

- Muddle blackberries, sage leaves, and simple syrup in a highball glass.
- Add ice, then pour in vodka, amaretto, cassis, and orange juice.
- Mix well and add a splash of soda water.
- Serve.

MANHATTAN CARAMELLATA

3½ ounces premium bourbon

½ ounce Grand Marnier

¼ ounce maple syrup

Ice

1 mint leaf, for garnish

- Combine all the ingredients in a shaker.
- Shake well and serve up or on the rocks, garnished with a mint leaf.

WATERMELON MOJITO

4 large mint leaves

1½ teaspoons sugar

Squeeze of lime

2 ounces watermelon juice (use your juicer, or puree watermelon in a blender)

Ice

3 1-inch cubes watermelon

Splash simple syrup

2 ounces rum

Splash soda water

- In a highball glass muddle mint leaves, sugar, squeeze of lime, and watermelon juice.
- Add ice to the glass.
- In a shaker, combine watermelon cubes, simple syrup, and rum.
- Shake well and pour over contents in the highball glass.
- Mix well and add a splash of soda water.
- Serve.

BLUEBERRY VANILLA MARTINI

- In a shaker, muddle blueberries and 7-Up.
- Add ice, vodka, simple syrup, and a squeeze of lemon.
- Shake well and serve up or on the rocks, garnished with a lemon wheel or extra blueberries.

5 fresh blueberries, plus extra for garnish (optional)

Splash 7-Up

Ice

3½ ounces vanilla vodka

¼ ounce simple syrup

Squeeze of lemon

Lemon wheel, for garnish

BASIL LIME GIMLET

- Combine all ingredients in a shaker.
- Shake vigorously and strain into a martini glass.
- Float a basil leaf in the gimlet and serve.

3 ounces premium vodka

1½ ounces freshly squeezed lime juice

½ ounce simple syrup

3 large basil leaves, torn

Ice

1 small whole basil leaf, for garnish

TUSCAN MARGARITA

- Combine all ingredients in a shaker.
- Shake well and serve up or on the rocks, garnished with a lime wedge.

1½ ounces tequila

½ ounce Cointreau

½ ounce Grand Marnier

1 ounce freshly squeezed lime juice

¼ ounce simple syrup

Splash orange juice

Splash pomegranate juice

Ice

Lime wedge, for garnish

Chapter 5

TIME FOR THE
GREATEST HITS OF RADIUS

Have you ever had a dream come true? I have: Radius is the restaurant I always dreamed of but was unsure I would ever get to realize. Not that I thought I wouldn't ever be the owner of a restaurant, I just never thought I would get to be involved with one so good. Every component — food, wine, service, ambiance — are all in perfect balance. No one aspect overpowers or out-shines another.

From my business partners, Christopher Myers and Esti Parsons, to the hundreds of business associates and friends who have contributed to the restaurant's success, my list of thank yous could take hours to recite. They've all been part of shaping Radius's particular philosophy, its role in Modern French cooking, its national awards, as well as some wild tales.

When people hear "Modern French" they immediately want to know how it differs from traditional French cooking. Although based on the fundamentals of classic French cuisine, Modern French cooking incorporates a tremendous variety of ingredients and techniques from around the world. No spice or ingredient is off-limits; the trick is to gently introduce these items into what for centuries has been a very narrowly defined cuisine. For example, you might find curry in a Modern

French dish, but it would be used as a subtle background seasoning; you wouldn't see it on the menu featured prominently in something like the spicy Indian dish chicken vindaloo.

In Modern French cooking there is an emphasis on exposing or unearthing the flavor from products without altering them too much. By using infused oils, flavored and reduced juices, and seasoned broths, we try to highlight, rather than mask, the different components in a dish. These techniques also contribute to a more healthful style of eating, because dishes don't rely on the cream and heavy butter sauces that were once the hallmarks of French cooking.

Make no mistake, this not your father's nouvelle cuisine. In addition to new ingredients, new cooking techniques like slow roasting, olive-oil poaching, and *sous vide* are becoming more and more common in Modern French kitchens. There's always a nod to the classics, but at the same time there's a movement toward more pronounced flavors with more colorful, exacting presentations.

How does all this play in America? Ah America, where we won't eat rabbit or venison because those animals remind us of cartoon characters. Yet we love to eat corn, which the French think should be fed only to pigs. When translating a cuisine from one culture to the next, it's all a matter of perception. Here, no one wants to eat pigeon, so I have to call it *squab* to get it past a menu reader. And I had to forget about writing *confit of pork* on the menu at Radius; it wouldn't sell, but if I write *tender pork*, it flies out of the kitchen. The usual response from the guest is, "This is the most tender piece of pork I've ever had in my whole life — is it tenderloin?" No, I want to tell them, it's actually from the butt, I just happened to cook it for six hours on a very low temperature, completely submerged in duck fat. But if I allowed my servers to describe it that way, of course, we'd never sell a single order again.

America is still new to loving food in a serious way, and I really don't care what I have to call my dishes as long as my guests are enjoying themselves. I hope they find the cooking at Radius soulful and exciting. While it can be said that our approach to food is exacting, meticulous, and sometimes even minimalistic (by the way, that does not mean the portions are small), it is always meant to be appealing and direct. We want our guests to leave saying to themselves, "That was done so well. They obviously love what they do and where they do it. I can't wait to come back."

Meeting expectations can sometimes be difficult. If you only have one night, one meal in Boston, we want you to dine with us and feel like you made the right decision. Our goal at Radius is simple but hard to attain: Give our customers perfect dinners that they'll remember for a long time.

AMUSE BOUCHE \a-'myuz bush\ [Fr. amuse the mouth] 1 : a small bite before the meal begins 2 : greeting from the chef de cuisine.

The *amuse bouche* has become commonplace in upscale eateries, and it really is a two-edged sword. At Radius, our emphasis on hospitality naturally makes me want to send "a little something" to all my guests when they sit down to dinner; they've chosen to eat at my "house," and I want to extend a thank-you for coming over tonight. By definition, the amuse bouche is small, from one to three bites, and it is generally tart or slightly salty to prepare the diners' taste buds for the meal that is about to unfold. At the restaurant, I often prepare more than one amuse bouche in anticipation of my guests' dietary demands and preferences.

There's just one problem with the amuse bouche: People tend to scoff at it — it has certainly elicited its share of wisecracks at the restaurant. People often assume that because this gift from the kitchen is on the small side, it is a sign of the meager portions that are sure to follow. While I do not serve the gargantuan portions that so many American diners seem to expect when eating out, I've never heard of anyone leaving the restaurant hungry. Still, I can't help feeling sorry for the poor amuse bouche. Guests needn't mock it just because it's petite. It has a very specific job to do, and when left to do its work it really does get you ready for all the tastes that are about to come. Plus, it's free!

HAMACHI TARTARE

WITH WARM SCALLION COMPOTE AND CAVIAR

When guests decide to order the Chef's Tasting Menu at Radius, I aim to fill them with a sense of anticipation from the first bite. I want them to think, "I'm so glad we decided to leave things in the kitchen's hands, I can't wait to see what's next." This hamachi tartare never fails to produce that effect. The caviar pairs so well with the rich yellowtail, and because it's salty it awakens the palate. I have never really understood why cheese and crackers are so often served to whet the appetite; rich, creamy cheese just coats the taste buds, dulling them to the delicate nuances of the courses to follow.

NOTE If you cannot find fresh, sushi-grade hamachi (yellowtail tuna), fluke or snapper make excellent substitutes.

Makes 6 "VIP" amuse bouche

FOR THE HAMACHI TARTARE
- Combine the hamachi with 1 teaspoon minced shallots, the thyme, ginger juice, lemon juice, and olive oil, and season with salt and pepper.
- Divide the tartare between six 2-inch ring molds that are 2½ inches tall.
- Press down and refrigerate up to one hour before serving.
- Just before serving, prepare the Scallion Compote.

FOR THE SCALLION COMPOTE
- Place a small sauce pot over high heat and allow it to get very hot.
- Add the scallions and cook 30 seconds, pressing down a few times with the back of a large spoon.
- Add the shallots and cook 1 minute.
- Add the butter and sugar, and season with salt and pepper.
- Remove from the heat, taste, and adjust the seasoning if needed.

TO SERVE
- While the compote is still warm, spoon ½ teaspoon of compote on top of the Hamachi Tartare and spread to cover completely.
- Place a teaspoon of caviar on top of the compote and gently spread to cover the scallions.
- Transfer the ring molds to the center of six small plates, carefully remove, and serve immediately.

FOR THE HAMACHI TARTARE

12 ounces sushi-quality hamachi, very finely diced

2 teaspoons minced shallots

1 large pinch fresh thyme, chopped

1 tablespoon ginger juice (use your juicer or substitute ¼ teaspoon grated fresh ginger)

Juice of half a lemon

1 ounce (2 tablespoons) extra-virgin olive oil

Salt and pepper

Scallion Compote (recipe follows)

6 teaspoons Osetra caviar

FOR THE SCALLION COMPOTE

1 cup finely sliced scallions

1 teaspoon minced shallots

1 teaspoon butter

1 pinch sugar

Salt and pepper

NEW ENGLAND SHELLFISH SALAD
WITH SPICY GAZPACHO WATER

4 large shrimp, unpeeled

1 1-pound lobster

10 small clams (see page 62 for a tip on cleaning clams)

2 ounces (¼ cup) water

3 ounces (6 tablespoons) extra-virgin olive oil

4 small scallops (use bay or sea scallops, whichever are freshest)

Salt and pepper, to taste

Juice of 1 lime

¼ zucchini, cut into small dice

1 tablespoon chopped fresh cilantro leaves

Gazpacho Water (recipe follows)

The Atlantic coastline near Boston is the source of an amazing array of seafood, and I can't help but feel obligated to take advantage of it. I have featured this salad in various forms on the Radius menu every summer, and it is always very popular, a refreshing way to enjoy the gifts from our local waters.

NOTE Shrimp always taste better if cooked with their shells left on, and even more flavor can be found if you cook and serve the shrimp head-on. This is true with just about all seafood. I always avoid buying shrimp that has already been peeled, especially if it has been frozen. The cooking time won't change just because the shells are still on; when the shrimp turns a light pinkish-orange color, they are finished.

Makes 2 first courses

- Prepare the gazpacho water (recipe on following page).
- Bring a large pot of water to boil, add the shrimp, and cook until they turn pink, 3 to 5 minutes (depending on their size). Remove with a slotted spoon, let cool, then peel, devein, and cut in half lengthwise.
- Using the same pot of boiling water, add the lobster and boil 6 minutes. Remove the lobster from the pot and transfer to a bowl of ice water. Chill. (Or have the lobster steamed by the guy at the fish counter.) Remove the meat from the claws, knuckles, and tail, and cut the tail in half lengthwise.
- Put the clams in a small sauce pot with 2 ounces (¼ cup) water. Cover the pot, place over high heat, and cook until the clams open. Let the clams cool, then remove from shells.
- Heat 2 tablespoons olive oil in a small sauté pan over high heat. Season scallops with salt and pepper, then sear on both sides until just cooked through, 1 to 2 minutes. Let cool.
- Combine the shellfish in a mixing bowl with the remaining olive oil, lime juice, zucchini, cilantro, salt, and pepper.
- Refrigerate until well chilled. Can be prepared to this point early on the day it will be served.
- Divide the shellfish salad between two large bowls. (For a really dramatic effect, use large martini glasses.)
- Pour the chilled gazpacho water over the shellfish and serve.

GAZPACHO WATER

Makes enough for 2 first-course servings of New England Shellfish Salad

- Coarsely chop the tomatoes, cucumber, jalapeño, red pepper, and onion.
- Transfer the vegetables to a food processor, add the cilantro, lime juice, and vegetable stock, and puree.
- Season with salt, pepper, and cayenne pepper, to taste.
- Pour the puree into a bowl lined with three layers of cheesecloth. Gather up the sides to form a pouch, then twist the ends of the cheesecloth and tie to create a pouch.
- Tie the pouch to a rack or post in the fridge, and place a pot underneath to catch the liquid that drips out. (This is best done in the fridge, but can also be done at room temperature.)
- Let the liquid drain for 4 hours, then wring out the pouch to extract the rest of the gazpacho water.
- Taste for seasoning and refrigerate until serving time. (This can be made ahead and frozen.)

4 tomatoes

1 cucumber

½ red jalapeño

½ red pepper

½ white onion

2 tablespoons chopped fresh cilantro leaves

Juice of 1 lime

8 ounces (1 cup) Clear Vegetable Stock (page 214)

Salt, pepper, and cayenne pepper

JUST A REGULAR GUY. . . I may be the chef and co-owner of a four-star restaurant, but I have to make two quick confessions:

1. At a very early age I realized girls thought it was pretty cool that I liked to cook.

2. For years I had a weakness for Steak-um sandwiches with hot peppers, hot sauce, ketchup, mayonnaise, and too much melted cheese on toasted onion rolls. I consumed them at any time of day, usually while leaning over the kitchen sink. My cravings were almost an obsession, but fortunately I outgrew them by about the age of 27. Rest assured I'm over that stage now; I have moved on. But I still often wonder if Paul Bocuse has ever realized the glorious pleasures a Steak-um sandwich has to offer.

HOS·PI·TAL·I·TY \häs-pə-ta-lə-tê\ *n, pl.* **-ties**

1. Cordial and generous reception of guests.

2. An instance of being hospitable. [ME hospitalite < OFr. < Lat. hospitalitas < hospitalis, of a guest. — see HOSPITAL.]

What makes for a great business relationship? Damned if I know the answer. Everyone tells you not to go into business with family or friends, but I have to disagree. So much time is spent at work, why go into business with people you don't particularly like? How much fun could you possibly have?

If just one story could perfectly illustrate why I am in business with Christopher Myers, it is this one.

First, you should know that important as good food may be to a restaurant's success, it is only a small fraction of the overall package. At Radius, your experience starts on the telephone when you make your reservation, and it does not end until the valet closes your car door and wishes you good night. In fact, we consider the valets an integral part of the evening, because they make the first and final impressions, often the lasting ones. Christopher is forever checking in with the valets, making sure things are going smoothly and asking what they've heard, since they often hear the guests' comments on the way out.

One busy Friday night Christopher came to the restaurant's front door as usual. He asked the valets how the night was going and noticed a dilapidated car parked in front of the restaurant. Dirty, dented, and rickety, it was really in rough shape, and it stuck out like a sore thumb from the shiny new BMWs, Mercedes, and Porches in the valet zone. We are not car snobs by any measure, but this automobile was one sad dog.

The valets informed Christopher that the car belonged to a young couple who requested that it not be taken to the garage because it was almost out of gas. The car had been running on fumes, they said, and they were afraid if it made the trip to the garage and back, there wouldn't be enough fuel to drive to the gas station after their meal.

Christopher asked for the valet ticket and the guests' names and quietly returned to the front desk. He spoke with Esti Parsons, our other partner, and learned the couple was celebrating their anniversary and were seated at table 21. Christopher nodded, then made his way through the dining room to greet diners before coming to the kitchen to say hello to me. He asked how table 21's meal was progressing and wanted to make sure I knew it was an anniversary dinner. Yes, I assured him, I knew. They were on their second of seven courses in the tasting menu. All was going well.

What Christopher did next has become something of a folk legend at our restaurants, and it really captures the spirit of what we are all about. He snuck back to the valet stand, gave one of the valets the keys to his own car, and said, "Follow me." Christopher drove the couple's jalopy to the gas station, escorted by the valet in case he ran out of gas. He filled up the tank, had the car washed, and returned to the valet parking lot. But here's the best part: He didn't tell a soul. He simply put a note on the steering wheel that read:

We hope you enjoyed your dinner at Radius.
No worries about the gas.
Sorry we did not have time to Simonize the tires.
Happy Anniversary
Michael, Esti, and Christopher

No bravado, no "look what I did," no mention at all, as if it was the most natural thing in world to do.

If you ask me, that is the real definition of hospitality. It is the reason for the restaurant's success, and it is at the heart of my business partnership and friendship with Christopher. At Radius, we focus on one guest at a time, one situation at a time, and we try to be prepared for anything. This couple has celebrated their anniversary with us ever since. Now, I'm not suggesting you drive up to our restaurants with an empty fuel tank in hopes of a free refill. Coffee is never a problem, but I can't make any guarantees about petrol. Christopher might be taking a rare night off, and I wouldn't want to see you ending up stranded on the side of the road!

JAPANESE OCTOPUS
WITH SWEET YELLOW PEPPERS, PICKLED SHALLOTS, & SPICY CITRUS JUICE

If I had to choose, this might well be my single favorite Radius dish. It really does have everything going for it: It is light, simultaneously sweet and spicy and tart, and it has great texture, without any element being overpowering.

NOTE Japanese octopus, called *tako*, really does work best for this recipe. You can buy it at Japanese or some Asian specialty stores (pick up togarashi and sriracha chili sauce while you're there). If you can't find tako, regular fresh octopus can be substituted — boil it gently for a couple hours until tender, and let cool before slicing. Both tako and regular octopus must be sliced as thinly as possible, otherwise they can be quite chewy.

Makes 4 appetizers

- In a mixing bowl, combine the octopus, haricots verts, togarashi, and Sweet Yellow Peppers.
- Drizzle 2 ounces (4 tablespoons) Spicy Citrus Juice into the octopus mixture and toss well. (The salad may be prepared to this point and refrigerated for up to 30 minutes.)
- Divide the octopus salad between four shallow bowls.
- Arrange four to five Pickled Shallot rings on top of each salad.
- Pour a scant 2 ounces (4 tablespoons) Spicy Citrus Juice over the top of each salad, garnish with microgreens, and serve.

1 pound tako, cut into really thin round slices

6 tablespoons paper-thin rounds of blanched haricots verts

1 pinch togarashi (see page 24; cayenne pepper can be substituted)

1 recipe Sweet Yellow Peppers (recipe follows)

1¼ cup Spicy Citrus Juice (recipe follows)

16 to 20 rings Pickled Shallots (recipe follows)

Microgreens, for garnish (optional, baby mâche can be substituted)

SWEET YELLOW PEPPERS

This recipe can be prepared up to three days in advance and refrigerated.

Makes ⅓ cup, enough for 4 Japanese Octopus appetizers

- Combine all of the ingredients in a small sauté pan and bring to a boil over high heat.
- Reduce heat to medium and simmer until the pepper starts to soften, about 5 minutes.
- Cool and reserve.

1 yellow pepper, diced into perfect ¼-inch dice

½ teaspoon sugar

½ teaspoon rice wine vinegar

½ ounce (1 tablespoon) canola oil

2 ounces (4 tablespoons) water

PICKLED SHALLOTS

4 ounces (½ cup)
red wine vinegar

¼ cup sugar

2 ounces (¼ cup) water

1 ounce (2 tablespoons) red
beet juice

2 shallots, thinly sliced and
separated into individual rings

This recipe can be made a week in advance and the shallots refrigerated.

NOTE To make beet juice, take a small beet, peel it, and put it through a juicer. If you don't have a juicer, boil a few beet slices with the vinegar mixture and let steep overnight to color the shallots.

Makes 6 to 8 tablespoons, enough for 4 Japanese Octopus Appetizers

- Bring the vinegar, sugar, water, and beet juice (or beet slices) to a boil over high heat and cook for 1 minute.
- Place the shallot rings in a small bowl or cup.
- Pour the vinegar over the shallots. Cover and refrigerate overnight.

SPICY CITRUS JUICE

1 ounce (2 tablespoons)
lemon juice

2 ounces (4 tablespoons)
lime juice

3 ounces (6 tablespoons)
tangerine juice

3 ounces (6 tablespoons)
Ruby Red grapefruit juice

2 ounces (4 tablespoons)
blood-orange juice (if
blood oranges are not in
season, substitute regular
oranges)

1 ounce (2 tablespoons) rice
wine vinegar

½ teaspoon Thai sriracha
chili sauce

1 pinch togarashi (see page 24;
cayenne pepper can be
substituted)

2 teaspoons sugar

This juice keeps for up to two days in the refrigerator.

Makes 1¼ cups, enough for 4 Japanese Octopus Appetizers

- Combine all of the ingredients in a mixing bowl and refrigerate.
- Before serving, adjust sweetness and amount of spice by adding more sugar and togarashi, if needed.

SOUPE DE POISSONS

We serve this soup all year long at Radius. It never comes off the lunch menu, and there are guests who order it every time. I think the perfect balance of flavors is what makes it so popular. It is a creamless soup that has a creamy, rich consistency, and I love the hint of spice the crushed red pepper flakes give to the finished dish. Traditionally, this soup is served with toasted bread, rouille, and grated Gruyère cheese. It's a classic combination of flavors, but I find it too filling to serve as a first course; I never seem to have enough room for the entrée to come.

NOTE: Since this soup is pureed, the vegetables and fish do not need to be cut with geometric precision, just roughly chopped.

Makes 5 quarts (can be prepared up to a day ahead; leftovers freeze well)

- Heat the olive oil and garlic in a large soup pot over high heat until the garlic is a light golden brown.
- Add fennel, carrots, leeks, and onions and cook for 3 minutes, stirring occasionally.
- Add the white wine and cook for 3 minutes.
- Add saffron and the tomatoes and cook for 1 minute.
- Add the salt, white pepper, and crushed red pepper flakes and cook for 1 minute.
- Add the fish stock.
- Bring the soup just to a boil, then reduce heat to medium-low and simmer, uncovered, for 1 hour.
- Add the fish and simmer 5 minutes.
- Remove from heat. Allow the soup to cool 15 minutes or so, and then puree in batches in a high-speed blender until smooth and creamy.
- Add the lemon juice and adjust seasoning. If the soup is too thick, add a little water or stock.
- Reheat gently and serve.

4 ounces (½ cup) extra-virgin olive oil

2 cloves garlic, sliced

4 bulbs fennel, trimmed and chopped into medium-size pieces

3 carrots, peeled and chopped into 1-inch pieces

3 leeks, white part only, well-rinsed, and chopped into 1-inch pieces

2 white onions, cored and cut into medium dice

6 ounces (¾ cup) dry white wine

1 large pinch saffron

6 ripe plum tomatoes, cut into small pieces

Salt and white pepper

1 heaping teaspoon crushed red pepper flakes

4 quarts Fish Stock (page 217)

18 ounces fresh, white-fleshed fish fillets, cut into 1-inch pieces (halibut or cod fillets are best)

Juice of 1 lemon

OLIVE OIL–POACHED DUCK

WITH SPINACH FONDUE, CHANTERELLE MUSHROOM RAGOUT, AND STAR ANISE

This recipe was inspired by an episode of the television program *Iron Chef*, which I watched one late night with my business partners, Christopher Myers and Esti Parsons, while devouring excessive amounts of Chinese take-out. One of the Iron Chefs took the secret ingredient, duck, and poached it for just 45 seconds in olive oil that was barely hot, a mere 105°F! He called this "Duck Sashimi" and paired it with a bunch of ingredients none of us had ever seen before. While duck sashimi would be a really, really tough sell in America, I was intrigued by the idea of giving duck a quick drop into barely simmering fat. I started to experiment. Not only did the results end up on the Radius menu, the dish became so popular I had to put it in this book.

NOTE You can buy a blend of canola and olive oils in many supermarkets. If you can't find it, make your own by using about 80 percent canola and 20 percent olive oil to poach the duck breasts.

ANOTHER NOTE You will need a meat thermometer to measure the temperature of the oil.

Makes 4 entrées

- Remove duck breasts from the refrigerator 5 minutes before the cooking is to begin.
- Place a 9 x 13-inch baking dish on the stovetop over very low heat.
- Pour enough oil into the pan to completely cover the duck breasts when they are added.
- Heat the oil to 140°F. Season the duck breasts with salt, pepper, thyme, and rosemary.
- Carefully submerse the duck breasts in the heated oil and cook for 8 minutes for medium-rare (or cook longer, as desired).
- While the duck is cooking, reheat the Spinach Fondue and the Chanterelle Mushroom Ragout over medium heat.
- Once the breasts are cooked, remove them to a wire rack and let the excess oil drain for 1 minute.
- Place 2 tablespoons Spinach Fondue on each of four dinner plates and use the back of a ladle to spin the mixture out into a 4- to 5-inch circle.
- Place a large spoonful of Chanterelle Mushroom Ragout in the center of each circle.
- Slice each breast into five or six pieces and fan out over the mushrooms.
- Spoon about ½ tablespoon of Star Anise Vinaigrette on and around the duck.
- Garnish with microgreens or chiffonade of scallions, if desired, and serve.

4 6-ounce boneless duck breasts (skin removed)

Blended olive oil and canola oil (for poaching, enough to cover the duck breasts, about 3 quarts for a 9 x 13 inch pan)

Salt and pepper

2 pinches fresh thyme, chopped

2 pinches fresh rosemary, chopped

½ cup Spinach Fondue (recipe follows)

1 cup Chanterelle Mushroom Ragout (recipe follows)

1 ounce (2 tablespoons) Star Anise Vinaigrette (recipe follows)

Microgreens or chiffonade of scallion, for garnish (optional)

SPINACH FONDUE

Makes about 1 cup, enough for 4 Olive Oil–Poached Duck entrées

2 heaping cups fresh spinach

½ cup Italian parsley leaves

2 cups heavy cream

1 ounce (2 tablespoons) butter

Salt and white pepper

- Blanch the spinach for 30 seconds in lightly salted boiling water. Drain, shock in ice water, and wring out excess liquid.
- Repeat the blanching process with parsley leaves. Drain, shock in ice water, and wring out excess liquid.
- Heat the heavy cream in a small sauce pot over high heat and reduce to about ½ cup. Let cool for 5 minutes.
- Combine all of the ingredients in a high-speed blender and puree until smooth and fluffy. Add a few drops of water if puree seems too stiff or does not move easily in the blender.
- Adjust seasoning and reserve. Can be refrigerated up to two days and then reheated before using. Freeze any leftovers.

CHANTERELLE MUSHROOM RAGOUT

Makes 1 cup, enough for 4 Olive Oil–Poached Duck entrées

1 tablespoon butter

2 tablespoons chopped shallots

1 cup chanterelle mushrooms, sliced in half

½ ounce (1 tablespoon) fresh lemon juice

2 ounces (¼ cup) water

1 pinch fresh dill, chopped

1 pinch fresh thyme, chopped

1 tablespoon crème fraîche

Salt and pepper

- Heat the butter in a sauté pan over high heat.
- When the butter is melted, add the shallots and sauté for 1 minute.
- Add the mushrooms and sauté for 2 minutes.
- Add the lemon juice and water, reduce the heat to medium, and cook for 1 minute.
- Add the dill, thyme, and the crème fraîche.
- Season with salt and pepper and reserve. (It's okay if the ragout is a little soupy; any excess liquid will be reduced during reheating.)

STAR ANISE VINAIGRETTE

Makes ¾ cup, enough for 4 Olive Oil–Poached Duck entrées

7 ounces (¾ cup plus 2 table-spoons) balsamic vinegar

1 large piece star anise

4 ounces (½ cup) canola oil

1 tablespoon minced shallots

1 tablespoon thinly sliced chives

1 pinch fresh thyme, chopped

Salt and pepper, to taste

- Simmer the balsamic vinegar in a small sauce pot until reduced to 2 ounces (¼ cup).
- Place the star anise in a dry sauté pan and toast over high heat for 30 seconds. Let cool, then crush into a powder.
- Combine all ingredients in a small bowl and whisk gently to combine. This is a "broken" vinaigrette; you want the oil and vinegar to remain separated.
- Refrigerate any leftovers, and use on salads, roasted squab, or meaty fish.

ROASTED SQUAB

WITH BRUSSELS SPROUT LEAVES, SMOKED BACON, AND SPICED BROTH

FOR THE SQUAB

8 ounces (1 cup) Spiced Broth (recipe follows)

2 ounces (¼ cup) canola oil

4 Statler-cut squab breasts, skins left on (see note on page 136)

Salt and pepper

1 teaspoon butter

1 pinch fresh rosemary, chopped

1 pinch fresh thyme, chopped

FOR THE BRUSSELS SPROUTS & SMOKED BACON

16 to 20 Brussels sprouts. Core, separate leaves, and blanch in salted water for 2 minutes.

1 teaspoon butter

1 teaspoon minced shallots

1 tablespoon finely diced rendered bacon

1 heaping tablespoon very finely diced carrot

Salt and pepper

1 tablespoon crème fraîche

1 pinch fresh rosemary, chopped

1 pinch fresh thyme, chopped

I often prepare this squab for guest-chef dinners, because I think it clearly illustrates our cooking style at Radius, and it lets us show off a little, too. Squab breasts make an ideal portion for a tasting menu, and the ingredients in this recipe combine to leave you with full flavors but not a full belly. For some reason, this particular member of the poultry family is a hard sell at the restaurant. I like to list the farms that raise these plump, well-fed birds so that no guest might mistake what's on the plate with what's hanging out on a statue in the park. These squab were raised for your dining pleasure.

NOTE Squab has the best flavor when served medium-rare. Cooked too much past medium, it starts to taste like liver.

Serves 4 (as an appetizer or part of a larger dinner)

FOR THE SQUAB

- Preheat the oven to 300°F.
- Bring Spiced Broth to a simmer in a small saucepan over low heat.
- Heat the canola oil in a large sauté pan.
- When the oil is hot, season the squab breasts with salt and pepper and place skin-side down in the pan. Lower the heat to medium-low and cook until the skins become deep golden brown and slightly crisp, about 4 minutes.
- Add the butter, rosemary, and thyme. Stir to melt the butter, and baste the flesh side of the bird a few times with the butter and herbs.
- Flip the squab over, remove the pan from the fire, and baste for 30 seconds.
- Transfer the squab to a roasting pan fitted with a wire rack to promote even cooking. Roast in the oven until medium-rare, about 8 minutes.
- While the squab is in the oven, prepare Brussels sprout leaves.

FOR THE BRUSSELS SPROUT LEAVES AND SMOKED BACON

- Melt the butter with the shallots in a small sauce pot over high heat and cook for 1 minute.
- Add the bacon, blanched Brussels sprout leaves, and carrot. Season with salt and pepper, and cook for 1 minute.
- Stir in the crème fraîche, rosemary, and thyme.
- Cook until the liquid from the crème fraîche is reduced completely, then taste and adjust seasoning.

TO SERVE

- Place a spoonful of the vegetable mixture in the center of four soup bowls.
- Arrange the squab, skin-side up, on the vegetables, ladle 2 ounces (¼ cup) of simmering Spiced Broth into each bowl, and serve.

SPICED BROTH

Leftovers can be frozen and used for soups or stews.

Makes 1 quart

- In a dry skillet, toast all of the seeds with the cinnamon and star anise over high heat for 2 minutes.
- Place the stock in a sauce pot and bring to a simmer.
- Add the toasted spices to the stock, reduce the heat to low, and simmer 3 minutes.
- Remove stock from the heat and steep for 30 minutes.
- Strain stock through a fine mesh sieve and adjust seasoning with salt and pepper.

½ teaspoon mustard seed

½ teaspoon fennel seed

½ teaspoon coriander seed

½ teaspoon cumin seed

1 cinnamon stick

2 pieces star anise

1 quart Rich-Roasted Poultry Stock (page 215)

Salt and pepper

SLOW-ROASTED PRIME RIB-EYE
WITH ROBUCHON POTATOES, HARICOTS VERTS, BABY CARROTS, AND RED WINE SAUCE

When we opened Radius, we knew we had to have a few dishes that would appeal to the steak and potato eater, and I knew that if I was going to have something so familiar on the menu, it had to be the best version available anywhere, perfect by any measure. Steakhouses are very popular in Boston, and my goal was to have our guests say the steak at Radius was the best they had ever eaten, even though the cooking at Radius couldn't be farther from steakhouse fare.

The technique that makes this steak extraordinary is actually a bit controversial. Most chefs and cookbooks instruct that meat should be seared at very high temperatures, then cooked at high heat and allowed to rest before serving. I could not disagree more. I think true success comes from cooking meats slowly, at very low temperatures.

My dear friend Craig Shelton, who is the unbelievably talented chef-owner of the Ryland Inn in Whitehouse, New Jersey, first introduced me to this concept. I spent some time working in his kitchen before moving to Boston, and we spent hours discussing the pros and cons of a technique we knew was not fully appreciated or understood in American restaurant kitchens. By lowering the temperatures of our oven, we concurred, we dramatically improved the quality of many different products.

Still, great techniques are nothing without great ingredients. Had it not been for Julia Child, this dish never would have become the success it is today. (It accounts for about 25 percent of our entrée sales.) No, Julia did not pass on some secret seasoning tip or foolproof cooking method. She introduced me to her butcher. The perfectly aged, well-marbled beef we buy from "Crazy" Ronny Savenor of Savenor Meats, in Boston, is the best steak I have ever tasted. All we really have to do at the restaurant is not ruin what he delivers to us, then round it out with the perfect accompaniment. I hope you'll find this to be "steak and potatoes at its finest."

Makes 2 entrées

FOR THE STEAKS
- Preheat the oven to 300°F.
- Heat canola oil in a large sauté pan over medium heat for 30 seconds.

directions are continued on following page

FOR THE RIB-EYE STEAKS

2 ounces (¼ cup) canola oil

2 9-ounce prime rib-eye steaks (ask the butcher to remove the "flap" before portioning)

Salt and pepper

1 pinch fresh thyme, chopped

1 pinch fresh rosemary, chopped

1 tablespoon butter

1 cup Robuchon Potatoes (recipe follows)

4 ounces (½ cup) Red Wine Sauce (page 217)

Parsley Oil, optional (page 216)

1 teaspoon finely diced tomatoes, optional

Fresh chervil sprigs, optional

FOR THE VEGETABLES

1 tablespoon butter

½ cup haricots verts, halved and blanched

8 baby carrots, halved lengthwise and blanched

6 pearl onions, peeled and blanched until just tender

Salt and pepper

1 pinch fresh thyme leaves, chopped

1 pinch fresh rosemary, chopped

1 teaspoon fresh lemon juice

- Season the steaks with salt and pepper and place in the pan. The pan should not be very hot. You do not wish to sear the meat; it shouldn't even sizzle.
- Cook the steaks for 1 minute on each side, then add a pinch each of thyme and rosemary.
- Add the butter to the pan and tilt the pan toward you to help distribute the butter. Baste the steaks with the melted butter and herbs.
- Flip the steaks once more, and baste again.
- Transfer the steaks to a roasting pan fitted with a wire rack and place in the oven for about 20 minutes for medium-rare.
- Remove the steaks from the oven and allow to rest for at least 10 minutes.
- While the steaks rest, gently reheat the Robuchon Potatoes and the Red Wine Sauce.
- Return the steaks to the oven to reheat for 3 to 4 minutes while you prepare the vegetables.

FOR THE VEGETABLES

- Melt the butter in a sauté pan over medium-high heat. Add the haricots verts, carrots, and onions and sauté until heated through.
- Season with salt, pepper, and a pinch of thyme and rosemary. Add a drop of lemon juice and taste for seasoning.

TO SERVE

- Place ½ cup Robuchon Potatoes in the center of each of two large dinner plates. Using the back of a ladle, spin out the potato puree into a perfect circle (as you would spread tomato sauce on a pizza).
- Divide the vegetables between the two plates, spooning into the center of the potato puree.
- Arrange the steaks on top of the vegetables.
- Spoon Red Wine Sauce around the edge of the potato puree.
- Garnish with Parsley Oil (optional), chervil sprigs, and finely diced tomatoes.

ROBUCHON POTATOES

2 pounds baking potatoes, unpeeled

3 tablespoons salt

8 ounces (1 cup) whole milk

1 cup unsalted butter, cut into small pieces

NOTE Robuchon's original recipe calls for equal parts potato and butter. However, he uses a potato (called *la ratte*) that is unavailable in most supermarkets, so I altered the recipe a bit for American home cooks. I hope Chef Robuchon does not mind my tinkering with his recipe for *pommes puree*. Any leftovers can be refrigerated and then gently reheated for another meal, but this is probably a moot point, since everyone always asks for seconds whenever I make these.

Makes enough for 2 Slow-Roasted Prime Rib-Eye entrées, plus seconds

- Preheat the oven to 250°F.

- Place the potatoes (in their jackets) in a large pot, cover by an inch with cold water, add the salt, and bring to a boil.
- Reduce heat to maintain a low boil, and cook until the potatoes are tender when pierced with a knife, about 30 minutes.
- Drain the potatoes. Peel as soon as they are cool enough to handle.
- Pass the potatoes through a food mill, arrange on a baking sheet, and place in the oven for 15 minutes to dry out.
- Meanwhile, heat the milk to a simmer in a small sauce pot and set aside.
- Transfer the potatoes to a medium sauce pot, place over moderate heat, and incorporate the butter a few pieces at a time, stirring with a wooden spoon.
- Slowly add the milk to the potatoes in a steady stream, continuing to stir.
- Pass the potato mixture through a *tamis* or *chinois*. (If you don't have either of these, you can use a sieve, but the potatoes won't have the same silky texture.)
- Adjust the seasoning with salt, if needed.
- Keep potatoes in a warm spot until you are ready to reheat them and serve.
- The potato puree should be much creamier and looser than regular mashed potatoes.
- These potatoes will keep for several days; serve leftovers with braised or roasted meats.

A FEW WORDS ABOUT JOEL ROBUCHON Joel Robuchon is a French chef who until his retirement in the late nineties was considered the greatest working chef in the world. His restaurants, Jamin and Joel Robuchon, both received three Michelin stars. He came out of retirement in 2003 to open L'atelier de Joel Robuchon in Paris, where many of the dishes that made him so revered can still be sampled, like this potato puree.

One of my favorite cookbook authors, Patricia Wells, wrote several cookbooks with Chef Robuchon, including *Simply French*, which is required reading for the Radius kitchen staff. Robuchon's meticulous eye for detail, including steps many might think trivial or unimportant, such as putting whole herbs in his salads rather than just using chopped herbs in the vinaigrette, set him apart from other chefs — and these are details I want my cooks to be aware of too. In *Simply French*, Robuchon writes, somewhat sarcastically, "I made my reputation making mashed potatoes and salad." Yet he manages to elevate both to such a level that "mashed potatoes and salad" does not do them justice. If you ask me, he deserves a lifetime achievement award, not for his multi-starred restaurants, but for taking such humble ingredients and turning them into something so sublime.

ROASTED CHICKEN

WITH BARLEY, ROOT VEGETABLES, AND CHICKEN-TARRAGON JUS

FOR THE
CHICKEN-TARRAGON
JUS

1½ cups Rich-Roasted Poultry
    Stock (page 215)

A few sprigs tarragon

Salt and pepper

FOR THE
CHICKEN

2 ounces (¼ cup) blended olive
    oil (see page 127)

2 Statler-cut chicken breasts,
    skins left on

Salt and pepper

1 pinch fresh thyme, chopped

1 pinch fresh rosemary,
    chopped

1 tablespoon butter

This roasted chicken has been among the top ten greatest hits at Radius since the day we opened, perhaps because it starts with such common ingredients and elevates their flavors so dramatically. Although so much Swiss-movement, precision dicing might seem overwhelming, this dish isn't all that difficult. Just read through the recipe completely and have all the ingredients ready before you start to cook.

NOTE If for some reason the bag broke on your barley and you lost the cooking directions, or if you stock up on stuff like barley in the bulk section of your supermarket and never had instructions to begin with, follow this easy cooking method: Place the barley in a large pot with plenty of lightly salted water (barley does not need to be soaked overnight). Bring to a boil over high heat, then reduce heat to medium and cook until tender. Quick-cooking barley takes 20 to 30 minutes, regular pearl barley needs about an hour. One cup of uncooked barley yields about 4 cups cooked.

ANOTHER NOTE Statler-cut, also known as French-cut, refers to a boneless poultry breast with the skin left on. The wing joint is also left on, but the wing tip is cut off at the "elbow." The meat pulls back from the bone that remains, creating an attractive presentation.

Makes 2 dinners

FOR THE CHICKEN-TARRAGON JUS
- In a small sauce pot over high heat, reduce the poultry stock to about 6 ounces (¾ cup).
- Place the tarragon in the stock and steep for 15 minutes.
- Season with salt and pepper.
- Taste for seasoning, strain through a fine-mesh sieve, and keep hot while preparing the chicken.

FOR THE CHICKEN
- Preheat the oven to 300°F.
- In an ovenproof sauté pan, heat the olive-canola oil over high heat.
- Season the chicken breasts with salt and pepper.
- Place the chicken, skin-side down, in the pan and lower the heat to medium-low.
- Cook until the chicken skin becomes golden brown, 7 to 8 minutes.
- Add the thyme, rosemary, and butter. Swirl the pan to help melt the butter, then baste the chicken a few times with the butter and herbs.
- Turn the chicken over, then place the pan in the oven and roast for 15 minutes, basting every 5 minutes or so.
- Meanwhile, prepare the barley and root vegetables.

FOR THE BARLEY AND ROOT VEGETABLES

- Melt the butter over high heat in a medium sauté pan.
- Add the shallot and cook for 1 minute.
- Add the diced root vegetables and squash, stir to combine, and lower the heat to medium.
- Sprinkle in the sugar and cook for 4 to 5 minutes, stirring occasionally, until the vegetables are cooked but not mushy.
- Stir in the cooked barley.
- Add the thyme and rosemary. Simmer 2 minutes, then season with salt and pepper.
- Add the lemon juice and set aside in a warm spot while the chicken finishes cooking.

TO SERVE

- Divide the barley and vegetable mixture between two shallow bowls.
- Place the chicken, skin-side up, on top of the barley and vegetables.
- Ladle half the heated jus into each bowl and serve.

FOR THE BARLEY & ROOT VEGETABLES

1 tablespoon butter

1 teaspoon minced shallot

2 tablespoons small-diced celery root

2 tablespoons small-diced carrot

2 tablespoons small-diced turnip

2 tablespoons small-diced rutabaga

2 tablespoons small-diced butternut squash

1 pinch sugar

1 cup cooked pearl barley (see note)

1 pinch fresh thyme, chopped

1 pinch fresh rosemary, chopped

Salt and pepper

Juice of ¼ lemon

CRÈME BRÛLÉE

8 ounces (1 cup) whole milk

3 cups plus 3 tablespoons heavy cream

6 ounces (¾ cup) sugar (half to be dissolved in milk and cream, half added to egg yolks)

2 Tahitian vanilla beans

7 egg yolks

1 pinch salt

10 ounces (1¼ cups) turbinado sugar, approximately

Crème brûlée has been on the menu since the day Radius opened, and it truly is the best version I have ever tasted. The recipe belongs to pastry chef Paul Connors, with whom I had the privilege of working in New York City and in Boston before he moved on to the Midwest. Paul and I both agree that crème brûlée should only come in one flavor: vanilla. If you want to make another flavor, call it something else.

Serves 6

- Combine milk, cream, and half of the regular sugar in a medium sauce pot.
- Split the vanilla beans and scrape the seeds into the milk mixture.
- Place over medium heat and bring almost to a boil, stirring a few times to dissolve the sugar.
- Whisk egg yolks and remaining regular sugar in a mixing bowl until the sugar is dissolved.
- Whisking constantly, slowly pour about a cup of the hot milk mixture into egg yolks in a thin stream.
- Whisk the tempered egg mixture into the remaining hot milk.
- Place the saucepan in a large bowl of ice water and let cool.
- Whisk in the salt.
- Preheat oven to 300°F.
- Pour custard into six 6-ounce ramekins.
- Place the ramekins in a baking pan lined with parchment paper or paper towels.
- Pour water into pan; it should come halfway up the sides of the ramekins.
- Cover the ramekins with an inverted baking sheet or aluminium foil.
- Bake until the custard has just set, 45 to 60 minutes, rotating the tray halfway through cooking. (Timing will vary depending on the shape of the ramekins and the temperature of the custard mixture before it is put in the oven.) To test for doneness, tilt the ramekins — the custard should no longer be liquid in the center, but it should jiggle. When the custards look about as firm as Homer Simpson's belly, they are done.
- Allow to cool completely, then refrigerate. Can be made up to 2 days in advance.
- Just before serving, sprinkle the turbinado sugar over the custards. Tilt the custards and lightly tap off excess sugar.
- Using a propane or butane torch, caramelize the sugar: Ignite the torch and adjust to a medium flame. Hold the torch close to the custards with the tip of the flame just touching the sugar, and slowly move it over the surface until the sugar is caramelized. Serve in the ramekins.

Chapter 6

TIME FOR A LITTLE THERAPY

COOKING IS GOOD FOR WHAT AILS YOU

This is the chapter for days when you are not in a hurry. We've already talked about dishes that are quick and easy and dishes that can be done in an hour and a half or so. Now it's time for some recipes that are meant to take your mind off things for a while; cooking can be great therapy for what ails you.

When I was a kid, nobody ever said, "I'm sooooo stressed." In fact, no one ever even used *stressed* in a sentence. These days stress seems to be a common, chronic condition. Studies about how it affects our physical health, our mental outlook, our sleep habits, our relationships — you name it — are all over the news. Wouldn't it be great if the next time someone asked, "How are you doing?" you could say, "I'm taking good care of myself, managing my time well, keeping my priorities straight."

Where's the fault in something that takes a really long time to develop, something that requires precision and real patience? This chapter is about cooking when the occasion is just that: cooking. Because cooking in and of itself is a healing act. Why not take a couple of hours, open up some wine, take a deep breath, turn on some music, and learn how to make slow-braised lamb shanks with barley risotto? Make today the day you say, "I'm going to try this." What's the worst thing that can happen — it doesn't work out? It's not like you lost your house in a poker game!

Just because some of these dishes take more time to prepare doesn't mean they're more complicated. Rolling gnocchi or stuffing ravioli may be time-consuming, but they're activities that are repetitive and relaxing. Using your hands can help you stop your mind from worrying, at least momentarily, about all the other things in your life that need tending to, or it can help you use your mind in a different way and maybe free you from any mental ruts you might have been stuck in.

Stretching pasta into sheets, running vegetable pearls through your fingers — the tactile pleasures of cooking are second only to the enticing scents of an active kitchen in terms of therapeutic value. Aromas are king: chicken roasting in the oven with lemon and herbs, mushroom soup simmering on the stove. . . . I've placed special emphasis here on dishes that will fill your home with pleasant, soothing smells — no cleaning stinky anchovy bones or cooking tripe in this chapter.

Although I mentioned cooking as a form of healing, please don't think I've been co-opted by the New Age crowd. I'm not talking about the smell of lit moonflower oil, I'm talking about things like cookies. Does anything smell better than walking into a house that smells of fresh-baked cookies? You think, "Where are they, and where's the milk?" It's aromatherapy. The smell makes you take a deep breath, sending more oxygen to the brain, and the body starts healing itself spontaneously. Oops, there's that word *healing* again. Well, what of it? We all need healing. Especially when we're all so damn busy.

HOMEMADE POTATO GNOCCHI

WITH PANCETTA, ESCARGOTS, VEGETABLE PEARLS, AND PARMIGIANO-REGGIANO

On those days when you need to be alone in the kitchen, with your hands doing all the work and your mind taking some time off, homemade gnocchi are just the thing. It really is worth taking the time to create something as wonderful as gnocchi. Kneading the dough, squeezing it between your fingers, rolling it into snakes — gnocchi are as much a pleasure to make as they are to eat, and your dining companions will definitely appreciate your efforts.

TRUC An 8-point scoop, available at kitchen stores, is actually just a tiny melon baller. Use it to carve the vegetables into the perfect uniform "pearls" that make this dish so aesthetically pleasing.

ANOTHER TRUC Placing the milled potatoes in a 250°F oven allows the excess moisture to evaporate. Less flour is required to form the dough, and the resulting gnocchi are tender and light as air.

NOTE *Pluche* is a French term for an herb sprig used as a garnish. The herb's leaves are often trimmed from the bottom of the stem — like a rose for a short bud vase.

Makes 6 first courses (plus additional gnocchi for the freezer)

FOR THE GNOCCHI

- Bake the potatoes in a 400°F oven until they can be easily pierced with a fork, about 40 minutes.
- Remove the potatoes from the oven and peel as soon as they are cool enough to handle.
- Pass the potatoes through a food mill and spread out in a thin layer on a baking sheet.
- Place pan in a 250°F oven for 15 to 30 minutes, until the potatoes have dried out. Do not allow them to brown.
- Remove the potatoes from the oven and let cool.
- Turn the potatoes out onto a work surface, make a well in the center, and incorporate the egg yolks.
- Add the flour, one cup at a time, working it in with your hands.
- Let the dough rest for 30 minutes under a moist cloth — this would be a great time to start those labor-intensive vegetable pearls.
- Add a few pinches of salt to the dough and incorporate.
- Roll a small piece of dough into a log, cut into ½-inch pieces (gnocchi), and drop into salted boiling water to test consistency. Add more flour if needed.
- Divide the remaining dough into four pieces, roll into logs, and then slice the logs into gnocchi using the back of the knife or a pastry cutter. Dust the work surface and gnocchi with flour to prevent sticking, if needed.

directions are continued on following page

FOR THE GNOCCHI

- 8 large Idaho potatoes (11 to 12 ounces each)
- 3 egg yolks
- 4 cups all-purpose flour (approximately)
- Salt

FOR THE SAUCE

- 2 tablespoons butter
- 3 tablespoons chopped shallots
- 6 tablespoons pancetta, diced and rendered (smoked bacon can be substituted)
- 30 small canned escargots, rinsed
- 1 large carrot, carved into pearls with an 8-point scoop
- ½ zucchini, carved into pearls with an 8-point scoop
- ½ yellow squash, carved into pearls with an 8-point scoop
- 4 ounces (½ cup) Vegetable or Chicken Stock (page 214)
- 1 pinch fresh rosemary, chopped
- 1 pinch fresh thyme, chopped
- Salt and pepper
- 6 tablespoons grated Parmigiano-Reggiano cheese
- 3 tablespoons finely sliced chives
- Chervil *pluches* for garnish (optional)

- You will need approximately 3 cups of finished gnocchi for six first courses. The remainder freeze really well — dust them lightly with flour, arrange in a single layer on a baking sheet, and freeze until firm. You can then transfer them to ziplock bags for storage, but spread them out in a single layer on a well-floured tray to defrost before boiling. (Or you can drop them straight from the freezer into rapidly boiling water.)

TO BOIL THE GNOCCHI AND PREPARE THE SAUCE
- Bring a large pot of salted water to a boil.
- Melt 1 tablespoon of butter over medium heat in a large saucepan.
- Add the shallots and cook for 1 minute.
- Add the cooked pancetta or smoked bacon.
- Add the escargots, vegetable pearls, stock, rosemary, thyme, salt, and pepper.
- Sauté over high heat for 2 minutes.
- Drop the gnocchi in the boiling water and remove with a slotted spoon after they have floated for 30 seconds.
- Add the gnocchi to the sauce and let simmer a minute or so, until the sauce is absorbed.
- Add the remaining 1 tablespoon butter, the cheese, and the chives. Taste and adjust the seasoning.
- Divide among six small shallow bowls, garnish with the chervil, and serve.

TO TEST THE CONSISTENCY OF THE GNOCCHI DOUGH Recipes for gnocchi almost always give an approximate amount of flour, since potatoes vary in size, moisture content, and their ability to absorb flour. The finished dough should not be sticky like bread dough, but it shouldn't reach the Playdough stage either. The only certain way to know you've got it right is to test a small sample before rolling out all the dough.

Bring a small pot of salted water to a boil. Pinch off a piece of dough and roll it on a floured surface into a small log, ½ inch in diameter. Using the back of a knife or a pastry cutter, cut the log into ½-inch pieces (the gnocchi) and drop them into the boiling water. Wait for the gnocchi to float to the surface, then continue to cook for another 30 seconds. Remove with a slotted spoon and taste for seasoning and texture. The gnocchi should be very light; if sticky and falling apart, work a touch more flour into the remaining dough and test again.

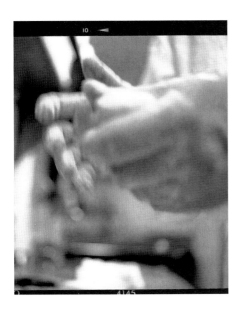

CASSOULET

(FRENCH WHITE BEAN STEW WITH LAMB, GARLIC SAUSAGE, & DUCK)

No comfort food manages to satisfy on as many levels as cassoulet. The aromas filling the house as it cooks away in the oven couldn't be more soothing, and when you crack into it on a cold winter night and open a great bottle of red wine, well, let's just say it actually makes it seem all right to live in a place where it snows eight months out of the year. As an added bonus, any leftovers can be heated again and again; they just keep getting better. Serve cassoulet with a light salad and some grilled bread (see truc on page 60), and don't forget to light a fire in the fireplace.

NOTE Cassoulet is a robust, filling dish, and it should only be served when the weather calls for a sweater and gloves. I once visited a restaurant here in Boston and they had cassoulet on the menu in July! What were they thinking? Hadn't they been outside?

Makes dinner for 6

- Preheat oven to 275°F.
- Season the lamb with salt and pepper.
- Heat the olive oil in a large ovenproof casserole over high heat. Add the lamb and sear until browned on all sides. Transfer to a platter and reserve.
- Roast the garlic sausages in the oven for about 10 minutes. Remove from the oven, allow to cool, and then cut into 1½-inch slices and reserve.
- Add the garlic, carrot, onion, and celery to the ovenproof casserole and cook over moderate heat on the stovetop for 2 to 3 minutes.
- Add the tomato paste and white wine, and cook for 2 more minutes.
- Add the lamb, beans, rosemary sprig, veal stock, and enough vegetable stock to cover the beans by about 1 inch.
- Cover the pan and place in the oven until the lamb is meltingly tender and the beans are cooked, 2 to 3 hours. Check occasionally, and add more vegetable stock if the beans are absorbing all the liquid.
- Remove the lid, mix in the reserved sausage and duck confit, and cook uncovered for 15 minutes.
- Adjust seasoning with salt, if needed. The beans will continue to absorb the liquid as they cool, so let the cassoulet sit if it seems too runny; it should be thick and creamy.
- Allow to cool for 30 minutes.
- If desired, sprinkle the bread crumbs over the cassoulet to create a golden crust. Place under the broiler until the bread crumbs become crisp and richly browned.

1 pound lamb stew meat, cut into 1-inch cubes

Salt and pepper

4 ounces (½ cup) pure olive oil

1 pound garlic sausages (pork or lamb)

1 clove garlic, thinly sliced

1 carrot, cut into medium dice

1 white onion, cut into medium dice

1 cup chopped celery

4 tablespoons tomato paste

8 ounces (1 cup) white wine

2 pounds white beans (French tarbais beans are traditional, but canellini can be substituted), soaked overnight in plenty of water

1 large sprig rosemary

1 quart Veal Stock (page 216)

2 to 3 quarts Clear Vegetable Stock (page 214)

8 ounces Duck Confit, removed from the bone (from 4 duck legs, page 218)

1 cup seasoned bread crumbs, optional (store-bought are fine)

ROASTED CHICKEN
WITH LEMON AND HERBS

What could be more comforting than the scent of a chicken roasting to perfection in the oven? Go for a full-day aromatherapy treatment: make gnocchi as a first course, and then serve this chicken as the entrée. You and your fellow diners will be ridiculously happy.

NOTE You can also use a whole chicken for this: Place it breast-side down on the lemon slices and herbs, and roast in a 275°F oven with the legs pointing toward the back of the oven. (This is the hottest part of the oven. Since the legs take longer than the breast, this will ensure that the breast does not overcook.) Roast a 4-pound chicken for about 1¼ hours, or until the juices run clear when pierced with a fork, basting frequently with the pan juices. Turn the chicken breast-side up, increase the oven temperature to 500°F, and return the bird to the oven to crisp the skin, about 10 minutes.

ANOTHER NOTE If you don't opt for the gnocchi as a first course, serve this chicken with Easy Roasted Vegetables (recipe follows). Since the cooking temperatures for these two dishes are different, prepare the vegetables first, then reduce the heat and roast the chicken. Return the vegetables to the oven for 10 minutes as the chicken finishes cooking.

Makes 4 portions

- Preheat the oven to 275°F.
- Heat the olive oil in a large sauté pan over high heat. (If you don't have a pan large enough to fit all four breasts without crowding, use two pans and divide the olive oil between them.)
- Season the skin side of the chicken breasts with salt and pepper.
- Carefully place the chicken skin-side down in the hot pan and reduce the heat to medium.
- Cook gently until the skin renders, becoming golden brown and crispy. Be patient — this may take 12 to 15 minutes.
- Meanwhile, cover the bottom of a roasting pan with the lemon slices. (Choose a high-sided pan that can hold the breasts without crowding.) Scatter the thyme sprigs, rosemary, and garlic over the lemon slices.
- When the chicken breasts are golden brown and crisp on their skin-sides, season them with salt and pepper and turn to cook briefly on the other side, about 30 seconds.
- Transfer the chicken breasts to the roasting pan, arranging them skin-side up on the lemon slices.
- Add the chicken stock, being careful not to pour it directly onto the chicken breasts.
- Place in the oven for approximately 18 minutes, until done (the juices will run clear when you poke the chicken with a roasting fork).
- Transfer the chicken breasts to a platter and keep in a warm place. Strain

directions are continued on following page

3 ounces (6 tablespoons) olive oil

4 Statler-cut chicken breasts, skins left on (see note on page 136)

Salt and pepper

1 lemon, sliced into thin rounds

3 sprigs fresh thyme

1 sprig fresh rosemary, broken into 4 pieces

1 clove garlic, smashed with the side of a knife but not chopped

8 ounces (1 cup) Chicken Stock (page 214)

2 tablespoons butter

the cooking juices through a fine mesh sieve into a small saucepan and reduce over high heat until only 3 ounces (6 tablespoons) remain.
- Whisk the butter into the reduced juices, check the seasoning, and add salt and pepper, if needed.
- Spoon the sauce on and around the chicken breasts and serve.

EASY ROASTED VEGETABLES
WITH WALNUTS

8 baby turnips, peeled and halved lengthwise (regular turnips can be substituted; cut them into 1½-inch wedges)

2 golden beets, peeled and cut into 8 wedges

8 whole baby carrots, peeled

8 Brussels sprouts, halved and blanched for 2 minutes

8 pearl onions, peeled and halved lengthwise

1 head of fennel, cut lengthwise into eighths

3 ounces (6 tablespoons) extra-virgin olive oil

Salt and pepper

1 pinch sugar

1 sprig rosemary, leaves removed from stalk but not chopped

4 sage leaves, coarsely chopped

1 cup coarsely chopped walnuts

Juice of 1 lemon

These roasted vegetables complement just about any grilled, roasted, or braised meat dish, but I wouldn't recommend serving them with fish, because root vegetables have a pronounced flavor that tends to overpower delicate fish. The vegetables I chose for this recipe create a pleasant balance of textures, colors, and flavors, and I love the crunch provided by the walnuts. But feel free to mix and match any of these vegetables according to what you have on hand or what looks good at the market.

TRUC By cutting all of these vegetables to about the same size, you ensure they will cook at the same rate.

ANOTHER TRUC Fifteen minutes before roasting the vegetables, place the empty roasting pan in the hot oven. Placing the vegetables in the hot pan gives them a quick sear and helps them caramelize.

Makes 4 side dishes

- Preheat the oven to 450°F.
- Place an ovenproof roasting pan in the oven for 15 minutes.
- Combine all of the vegetables and the olive oil in a large mixing bowl and season generously with salt and pepper.
- Add a pinch of sugar to help the vegetables caramelize, and toss well to coat evenly with the olive oil.
- Remove the heated roasting pan from the oven, add the vegetables, and shake the pan a few times to keep the vegetables from sticking.
- Roast, uncovered, for 20 minutes, stirring the vegetables occasionally to prevent sticking or burning.
- Add the rosemary and sage, and stir to combine.
- Check the vegetables for doneness — they should be almost tender.
- Continue to roast until the vegetables are cooked, but not mushy, then add the walnuts and adjust seasoning.
- Squeeze the lemon over the vegetables, stir to combine, and serve.

WILD MUSHROOM SOUP

WITH MORE MUSHROOMS, DILL, AND HAZELNUTS

Sometimes it's impossible to rush good food. This is one of those soups that takes some time to cook because the flavors need plenty of time to marry as the stock simmers. Smooth, creamy, and earthy, this soup will warm and nourish the body, and if your Japanese water fountain happens to be on the blink, the sound of this soup bubbling away on the stove will nourish your soul.

Makes 4 first courses, with plenty of soup left over for the freezer

FOR THE SOUP

- Melt the butter and olive oil in a large soup pot over high heat.
- Add the onion, carrot, and celery and stir well to combine.
- Continue cooking over high heat, stirring every 2 minutes or so, until the vegetables begin to caramelize, 8 to 10 minutes.
- When the vegetables are golden brown, stir in the tomato paste and red wine. Cook for 3 minutes, still over high heat.
- Add the fresh and dried mushrooms and stir for 1 minute. (You do not have to rehydrate the dried mushrooms.)
- Add the water or vegetable stock.
- Bring the soup to a simmer and then lower the heat to medium-low.
- Cook for 1½ hours, adjusting the heat if needed to maintain a steady simmer.
- Stir in the dill and rosemary, remove soup from heat, and let steep for 15 minutes.
- Add the heavy cream or crème fraîche and season with salt and pepper.
- Let soup cool for 15 to 30 minutes.
- Puree in batches in a high-speed blender until the soup is creamy and smooth.
- If the soup is too thick, thin with additional water or stock.
- Return soup to the pot and reheat gently over low heat before serving.

FOR THE GARNISH

- Melt the butter in a sauté pan over high heat.
- Place the wild mushrooms in the pan and sauté until cooked through, about 2 minutes.
- Squeeze the lemon juice over the mushrooms and season with salt and pepper.

TO SERVE

- Place a heaping spoonful of the warm mushroom garnish into the center of four soup bowls.
- Sprinkle each bowl with 1 teaspoon hazelnuts and a dill sprig.
- Ladle the hot soup over the mushrooms, drizzle with truffle oil, if desired, and serve.

FOR THE SOUP

2 tablespoons butter

2 ounces (4 tablespoons) extra-virgin olive oil

1 large onion, cut into medium dice

1 large carrot, peeled and cut into 1-inch rounds

2 celery stalks, cut into 1-inch pieces

3 tablespoons tomato paste

8 ounces (1 cup) red wine

3 pounds fresh mushrooms, sliced 1-inch thick (a mix of button and crimini is fine; no need to use anything fancier)

4 ounces dried mushrooms (porcini are best)

4 quarts water (use Clear Vegetable Stock, page 214, for an even more flavorful soup)

2 large dill sprigs

2 teaspoons chopped fresh rosemary

8 ounces (1 cup) heavy cream or crème fraîche

Salt and pepper

FOR THE GARNISH

2 tablespoons butter

2 cups assorted fresh wild mushrooms, sliced (use chanterelles, black trumpets, porcini, or whatever combination is available fresh)

Juice of 1 lemon

Salt and pepper

4 teaspoons coarsely chopped hazelnuts

4 fresh dill sprigs

Truffle oil (optional)

BRAISED LAMB SHANKS

WITH BARLEY RISOTTO

4 ounces (½ cup) canola oil

4 lamb shanks, left whole

  Salt and pepper

1 large white onion, cut into small dice

1 large carrot, peeled and cut into small dice

1 celery stalk, cut into small dice

1 clove garlic, thinly sliced

4 tablespoons butter

3 to 5 tablespoons flour

2¼ cups red wine

2¼ cups Chicken Stock (page 214)

2¼ cups milled tomatoes (see note on page 55)

3 pinches fresh rosemary, chopped

  Barley Risotto (recipe follows)

Preparing these lamb shanks is my idea of how to spend a perfect day in the kitchen: a little work at the beginning, and then the oven takes over with all the heavy lifting. As the lamb braises, it fills the house with intoxicating scents, and you don't have to do much but relax for a few hours. So here's the game plan:

1. Do a little extra prep work in the early afternoon.

2. Let a slow oven take over after the prep is done.

3. Take a nap while the house fills with enticing aromas.

4. Wake up, check the shanks, and get ready to serve dinner.

5. Take credit for all the hard work and hours spent cooking.

6. Remind guests about all that hard work and accept offer to be excused from doing dishes.

NOTE For this braise, the lamb shanks will be completely submersed in liquid, so choose a roasting pan that is deep enough to accommodate them.

TRUC Whenever you are braising, stewing, or cooking any meat submersed in liquid, there is one golden rule: Never allow the liquid to boil. It is fine to bring the liquid up to a boil, but once it reaches that point, turn the heat down to a very low simmer. Boiling dries out meats and makes them tough and rubbery. By cooking very slowly at low temperatures, meats will become fall-off-the-bone tender.

Makes 4 substantial entrées

- Preheat the oven to 300°F.
- Place the canola oil in a large, deep roasting pan and set over high heat on the stove top.
- Season the lamb shanks with plenty of salt and pepper and sear them in the hot oil until they turn golden brown on all sides, about 3 minutes.
- Transfer the shanks to a platter and add the vegetables and garlic to the pan. Stir to combine and cook for 2 minutes over high heat.
- Lower the heat to medium, add the butter, and heat until melted.
- Sprinkle in 3 tablespoons flour and stir, adding the remaining flour as needed, until the mixture resembles wet sand.
- Add the red wine and cook for 5 minutes, stirring frequently.
- Return the shanks to the pan.
- Add the chicken stock, milled tomatoes, and rosemary.
- Cover the pan with aluminum foil and place in the oven for 3 to 4 hours. Check every 30 minutes or so to make sure the liquid is very hot but never boiling, and reduce heat if needed.
- The lamb shanks are done when the meat has pulled away from the bottom

of the shank and at least 3 inches of bone is exposed. The meat will be very tender and almost falling off the bone.

- Allow the shanks to cool in the sauce for 20 minutes, skimming off any excess oil from the surface.
- If the sauce seems too thin, transfer a few cups to a sauce pot and reduce over high heat to thicken. Return the reduced sauce to the braising pan and place the shanks in a 250°F oven to keep warm until the risotto is ready.

TO PLATE THE WHOLE SHEBANG

- Spoon a generous serving of Barley Risotto onto each of four large dinner plates.
- Place the lamb shanks on the risotto and spoon some of the sauce over the top.

BARLEY RISOTTO

This is a play on the classic Italian risotto made with Arborio or Carnaroli rice. It is incredibly versatile, and vegetables such as turnips or *cavolo nero* (Italian kale) are welcome additions to the risotto. Barley is somehow more forgiving than rice, and this dish does not require quite as much stirring as traditional risotto. There's some, of course, but not nearly as much.

Makes 4 substantial side dishes

- Melt 1 tablespoon butter in a large sauce pot over medium-high heat.
- Add the shallot and carrot and cook for 2 minutes.
- Add the mushrooms and cook for 2 minutes, stirring occasionally.
- Add the rosemary, season with salt and pepper, and stir to combine.
- Stir in the cooked barley.
- Ladle in the chicken stock in three installments, adding more stock each time the barley absorbs most of the liquid. Stir occasionally and adjust the heat if needed to maintain a gentle simmer.
- When the barley has absorbed all of the stock, stir in the cheese and the remaining tablespoon of butter and simmer for 2 minutes.
- The risotto should have a creamy consistency. If it seems too dry, add a bit more stock or water, a knob of cold butter, and a little more cheese.
- Stir in the parsley.
- Taste and adjust seasoning.

2 tablespoons butter

1 shallot, minced

1 carrot, halved lengthwise, then cut into 1/3-inch-thick half-moons

10 button mushrooms, thinly sliced

1 pinch fresh rosemary, chopped

Salt and pepper

3 cups barley, cooked al dente (about 3/4 cup uncooked; see note on page 136)

4 cups Chicken Stock, plus additional if needed (page 214)

1/2 cup grated Parmigiano-Reggiano cheese

1 heaping tablespoon chopped Italian parsley

HOMEMADE RAVIOLI
WITH VEAL, PROSCIUTTO, AND SAGE

A classic "day in the kitchen" experience is to make homemade pasta and turn it into fabulous ravioli. This is a basic formula, excellent for your first foray into ravioli making. Once you gain a little experience and confidence you can branch out, both with the ingredients in the filling and the sauce you serve the ravioli with. Be as creative or traditional as you'd like; the possibilities are endless. What are you waiting for? Working with pasta truly is fun, and before you know it you might find yourself back in the kitchen, ready to do it all over again.

NOTE Toss these with Simple Tomato Basil Sauce (recipe follows), or the sauce from Buttered Noodles with Parmigiano-Reggiano and Sage (page 44), or pair with a light vegetable stock or cream-based sauce.

NOTE Fresh pasta is best the day it is made, but it can be kept in the refrigerator until the following day. Lay a kitchen towel on a sheet tray, dust with semolina flour, and arrange the ravioli in a single layer. Dust them with more semolina flour and cover with another kitchen towel. You can repeat with another layer and they will still keep their shape. Ravioli also freeze well (the exception is those with seafood fillings; their flavor suffers when frozen). To freeze uncooked ravioli, arrange in a single layer on semolina-floured baking sheets. Freeze until firm, and then transfer to ziplock bags for storage. For fresh ravioli, cooked the day they were made, plan on approximately 4 to 5 minutes boiling time. If you cook ravioli the day after making them, you will need an extra couple minutes. For frozen ravioli, remove them from the bag, drop them directly into boiling water, and cook for about 9 minutes. To test for doneness, cut a little piece from the edge of one of the squares and taste. The pasta should be al dente.

Makes 4 servings (6 ravioli per person) with leftovers for the freezer

FOR THE PASTA

- Pour 3½ cups flour into a mound on the work surface and make a well in the center.
- Whisk the eggs lightly in a mixing bowl to break up the yolks.
- Pour the eggs into the well.
- Using your fingertips or a fork, begin incorporating the flour into the eggs, working from the center to the outer edges of the mound.
- Add the olive oil and continue working the dough until it forms a ball.
- Knead lightly until smooth, adding flour as needed. Dough should be fairly stiff and no longer sticky.
- Let dough rest 15 to 30 minutes before rolling out.

FOR THE PASTA

3½ to 4 cups unbleached all-purpose flour

4 extra-large eggs

½ teaspoon extra-virgin olive oil

directions are continued on following page

FOR THE RAVIOLI FILLING

2 ounces (4 tablespoons) olive oil

8 ounces ground veal

6 slices prosciutto, finely diced

8 large fresh sage leaves, chopped

2 tablespoons chopped Italian parsley

4 tablespoons ricotta cheese (drained for 30 minutes in a colander to remove excess liquid)

2 tablespoons grated Parmigiano-Reggiano cheese

1 egg yolk

Salt, pepper, and crushed red pepper flakes, to taste

1 egg, whisked with a couple drops of water to make an egg wash for sealing ravioli

FOR THE SIMPLE TOMATO BASIL SAUCE

3 ounces (6 tablespoons) extra-virgin olive oil

12 to 15 large basil leaves, left whole

Salt and pepper

Crushed red pepper flakes

2 cups canned Italian tomatoes, milled (see note on page 55)

1 tablespoon butter

½ cup grated Parmigiano-Reggiano cheese (for garnish)

FOR THE FILLING

- Heat the olive oil in a sauté pan over medium heat.
- Add the veal and cook, stirring frequently, until browned and cooked through.
- Pour off excess fat and let cool.
- Transfer the veal to a mixing bowl and combine with the prosciutto, sage, parsley, ricotta, Parmigiano-Reggiano, egg yolk, salt, pepper, and crushed red pepper flakes.
- Taste for seasoning, and adjust if needed.

TO ASSEMBLE

- Divide the dough into four pieces. Use a rolling pin or the palm of your hand to flatten each piece into a rectangle.
- Working with 1 piece at a time, use a pasta machine to roll the pasta out as thin as possible into sheets, 6 inches wide. Start with the widest setting on the machine and progress to the thinnest, dusting the pasta sheets with flour to keep from sticking if needed. (If you don't have a machine, a rolling pin and a well-floured, flat surface will do the trick. Roll out the dough as thin as you can.)
- Trim both ends of the pasta sheets and cut into 6 x 12-inch rectangles.
- Place a rectangle of pasta lengthwise in front of you. Place scant teaspoonfuls of filling, spaced 2 inches apart, in two rows across the pasta sheet.
- Lightly brush the egg wash between the mounds of filling.
- Carefully place another pasta rectangle on top of the filling, and press down gently but firmly between the mounds to seal the two pasta layers together.
- Using a sharp knife or pizza cutter, cut between the mounds of filling to make 3-inch-square ravioli.
- Separate the squares and arrange them on a flour-dusted baking sheet, making sure they do not touch each other.
- Repeat with the remaining pasta sheets.

FOR THE SIMPLE TOMATO BASIL SAUCE

- Heat the olive oil and basil in a large sauté pan over high heat.
- Cook for 1 to 2 minutes, until the basil starts to crackle a bit.
- Season with 2 large pinches of salt, 1 large pinch of pepper, and 1 large pinch of crushed red pepper flakes.
- Add the milled tomatoes and cook over medium-high heat for 6 to 7 minutes, until the sauce thickens and begins to darken slightly.
- Stir in the butter and simmer until melted.
- Taste for seasoning, and add more salt, pepper, or crushed red pepper flakes if needed. This sauce should be boldly seasoned!

TO COOK THE RAVIOLI & SERVE

- Bring a large pot of lightly salted water to a boil.
- Adjust the heat under the Simple Tomato Basil Sauce to maintain a gentle simmer.

- Drop the ravioli into the water and cook for about 4 minutes. To test for doneness, cut a little piece from the edge of one of the squares and taste. The pasta should be al dente.
- Strain the ravioli and add them to the pan with the simmering tomato sauce.
- Add the grated parmigiano cheese and toss gently to combine, 1 to 2 minutes.
- Serve in individual bowls, or family-style, from a large platter.
- Pass additional Parmigiano-Reggiano at the table, if desired.

CHEWY CHOCOLATE CHUNK COOKIES
WITH MACADAMIA NUTS

These cookies are delicious and a snap to make. . . . they are only baked for 9 minutes so they remain soft and chewy. I think it almost goes without saying that the smell of cookies baking in your oven may be the most therapeutic, nostalgic, "takes me back to my childhood" smell we know. Simply, it soothes you.

Although there may be one or two of you who will disagree, I think all chocolate chip cookies should be chewy, never crispy. I know people can get pretty righteous about their cookies, but I've never met a chocolate chip cookie that was improved by being baked longer to make it crispier. Care to argue?

Will fill a small cookie jar

- Preheat oven to 375°F.
- Combine flour, salt, and baking soda in a small bowl.
- Using a mixer, cream the butter, both sugars, and vanilla extract until smooth.
- Add the eggs one at a time, mixing well after each.
- Add the flour mixture in ½-cup increments, mixing at low speed until incorporated.
- Stir in the chocolate chunks and macadamia nuts by hand.
- Drop rounded teaspoonfuls onto nonstick baking sheets or lightly greased sheet pans (try to refrain from eating dough).
- Bake until golden brown, about 9 minutes for chewy cookies. Let cool on the baking sheets, and get milk.

2¼ cups all-purpose flour

1¼ teaspoons salt

1 teaspoon baking soda

1 cup butter, softened

1 cup packed dark brown sugar

½ cup granulated sugar

1½ teaspoons vanilla extract

2 large eggs

2½ cups bittersweet chocolate chunks

1 cup coarsely chopped unsalted macadamia nuts

Chapter 7

TIME TO LOOK LIKE A PRO

WITHOUT PAINSTAKING DECADES
OF CULINARY APPRENTICESHIP

Nobody is less mechanically inclined than I am. I bought a weed whacker not long ago, and the only thing I had to do was put the stupid guard on, which would have taken anyone else about a minute. I'm embarrassed to say it took me half an hour: I just couldn't figure it out. I read and reread the directions. I may be inept at some things, but I do have perseverance. I said to myself: I'm not putting this down until I figure it out.

That's probably why I'm good at cooking; I don't give up until I get something right.

I'm talking about perseverance here, not patience — because, like anyone else would have done, I got mad when I couldn't put the thing together and have instant success. But you know what? The world didn't end. I eventually won the war with that damn contraption and now I have the pleasure of spending summer afternoons in my backyard whacking weeds. Oh, the pride of home ownership!

Think of how often you hear people say that they would do this or that if they could, but they can't. What they're really saying is "I don't want to fail, so therefore I won't try." And what I want to say is, "If you don't try, how do you expect to learn?" How can you expect to get good at anything if you aren't willing to make mistakes?

The first time you swung at a baseball, did you hit it out of the park? No, you missed the ball completely, guaranteed!

It's the same with cooking. Sometimes it takes a few misses before you get a hit. If your first attempts don't work, no big deal; keep at it. Many people at my cooking classes will say, "Oh no, I could never make that at home." Why not? The ingredients are just lying there, still and quiet like, waiting for your commands; you're the part of the equation that is alive and in control. If you pay attention and are willing to try, you'll have great success with these recipes.

In sports, coaches can be heard screaming, *"Go to the ball! Don't wait for it to come to you!"* The same advice goes for the kitchen. At my restaurants, I actually tell my cooks, "I want you to go to the food; I don't want the food to come to you." You're the one in control. You're the chef today.

Sound like a locker-room pep talk? That's my intent. I'm trying to get you psyched up for this chapter so you really can look like a pro. The good news is that these recipes will make it easy for you to look like you've spent years — okay, maybe weeks — apprenticing yourself at the finest culinary institutions in the world.

Beautiful plate presentations are an important part of looking like a pro. After all, you eat with your eyes first. But just as important are the ingredients you use and how you use them.

Some of the ingredients in this chapter might be unusual, even exotic, but that doesn't mean they're hard to work with. Take dashi, the key ingredient in a traditional Japanese noodle dish. You dissolve a certain amount of the dashi in boiling water. That's it! Middle-school home-ec stuff! When your guests inquire about this authentic creation, that's when you can make up a story about the last time you were traveling through Japan, learning cuisine and culture from your friend, Ikasa. Hey, the pros do it all the time.

And you won't need any fancy equipment to pull these recipes off, either. Most of the utensils required to create these professional-looking dishes are commonplace, or else they can be fashioned out of things like tuna cans and teaspoons that you already have in your cupboards and drawers. Your guests will murmur among themselves, wondering where you learned such artistry, and if they ask you outright, it's okay to tell them to buy this book.

The great thing about this chapter is that it'll help you prepare beautiful, delicious dishes that will look like they were hard to make, but you and I will know they really weren't.

PEA SOUP

WITH SPICY SHRIMP SALAD AND MINT

Peas are one of the rare vegetables that can actually taste better frozen than fresh. Because the sugars in peas start turning to starch as soon as they are picked, shell peas are at their sweetest and most tender right after harvest. Frozen peas are picked and packaged at their peak of ripeness, but fresh peas will grow tough and starchy if they sit around too long in the produce stall. So feel free to use frozen peas for this soup, or look for garden fresh ones at farmer's markets in spring and early summer. They should be firm, with no signs of withering, and the peas should not seem overly crowded in the pod.

NOTE This dish can also be served hot. Simply transfer to a pot and heat gently. Prepare the shrimp just before serving and place in bowls while still warm.

TRUC Choose a metal bowl for chilling the soup — metal conducts heat better than plastic. Set the container of soup in a larger bowl, pack ice around it, and pour cold water over the ice. Stir every few minutes to bring the heat down.

Makes 4 first courses

FOR THE PEA SOUP

- Put the vegetable stock and shallot in a sauce pot and bring to a boil over high heat.
- Add the peas (if using frozen peas, thaw first), spinach, and mint leaves and cook until the peas are tender, about 1 minute.
- Remove soup from heat and puree in three to four batches in a high-speed blender or food processor, adding 5 ice cubes to each batch.
- Transfer soup to a metal bowl and chill in an ice bath.
- Whisk in crème fraîche. Strain the soup through a fine-mesh strainer.
- Season with salt, white pepper, and sugar.
- The soup can be prepared a few hours ahead and refrigerated; it is best served the day it is made.

FOR THE SPICY SHRIMP SALAD

- Cook shrimp in a pot of boiling water until pink, about 3 minutes.
- Let cool slightly, remove the shells, and devein (see page 13).
- Slice shrimp into ½-inch pieces.
- Combine shrimp pieces with red onion, cilantro, lime juice, and togarashi.
- Season with salt and pepper.
- Refrigerate until serving time; this salad can be prepared earlier in the day.

TO SERVE

- Divide the shrimp salad between four soup bowls and top with mint sprigs.
- Bring the bowls to the table and pour the soup over the shrimp. To look like a pro, pour the soup from a decorative pot, maybe a teapot.

FOR THE PEA SOUP

- 4 cups Clear Vegetable Stock (page 214)
- 1 shallot, sliced
- 1½ cups freshly shelled peas (about 1½ pounds unshelled; frozen peas can be substituted)
- 1 loosely packed cup spinach, rinsed
- 10 fresh mint leaves
- 15 to 20 ice cubes
- 3 tablespoons crème fraîche
- Salt and white pepper
- 1 pinch sugar

FOR THE SALAD

- 12 large shrimp, in their shells
- ½ red onion, minced
- ½ teaspoon chopped cilantro
- Squeeze of lime juice
- 1 pinch togarashi (see note on page 24; cayenne pepper can be substituted)
- Salt and pepper
- 4 mint sprigs, for garnish

LAMB SALAD

WITH SWEET AND SPICY EGGPLANT, BABY GREENS, AND RED PEPPER SYRUP

Although my brother, Robert, is a real-estate broker, I often bring him along to special cooking events as my sous chef. I even bought him his own chef jacket, with "Li'l Schlow" embroidered on it. He's an excellent cook, and it's the only way we get to see each other. He once helped me prepare this lamb salad for a guest-chef dinner on a cruise ship. It was my first cruise, so I had no idea what to expect, but even I was taken aback when the cruise director informed me we would be preparing this for four hundred people. Just the two of us! It definitely tested the limits of Robert's brotherly love and his passion for cooking. I think he ordered take-out for a month after we returned home. I scaled this recipe to serve four, but you can work your way up to a banquet for four hundred, if you desire.

NOTE This recipe alone is worth the price of the juicer required for the Red Pepper Syrup. (Go ahead, buy one, you'll soon find it has countless uses, including my recipes for Hamachi Tartare and Japanese Octopus, pages 115 and 123.)

ANOTHER NOTE There is a gadget available at fine kitchen stores that closely replicates the classic quenelle shape, but it is not difficult to make quenelles the old-fashioned way, with two spoons: Scoop up a rounded mound of the salad with a tablespoon or teaspoon, depending on the size you prefer. Shape the top of the quenelle by inverting the bowl of the second spoon over the mound and scooping the salad out of the first spoon. Repeat a few times until the mound becomes a smooth, oval quenelle.

Makes 4 entrées

FOR THE SWEET AND SPICY EGGPLANT

- 2 ounces (4 tablespoons) olive oil
- 1 medium white onion, cut into small dice
- 1 large eggplant, cut into medium dice
- 2 ounces (4 tablespoons) honey
- 2 ounces (4 tablespoons) red wine vinegar
- ¼ teaspoon cumin powder
- ¼ teaspoon curry powder
- Cayenne pepper, to taste
- Salt and pepper, to taste
- 1 tablespoon chopped fresh cilantro

FOR THE EGGPLANT SALAD

- Heat the olive oil in a sauté pan over high heat.
- Add the onion and saute for 2 to 3 minutes.
- Add the eggplant and cook until lightly browned, stirring occasionally, 4 to 5 minutes.
- Turn down the heat to low and add honey, red wine vinegar, cumin, curry, cayenne, salt, and pepper. Continue cooking until the eggplant is tender but still moist.
- When the eggplant is finished, add the cilantro and combine.
- Adjust seasoning, if needed, to obtain a balance of sweet, spicy, and aromatic flavors.

directions are continued on following page

FOR THE
RED PEPPER SYRUP

8 ounces (1 cup) red bell pepper juice (approximately 3 peppers)

½ ounce (1 tablespoon) rice wine vinegar

Sugar

Salt and pepper

FOR THE
LAMB

2 12-ounce boneless lamb loins, trimmed of any excess fat

Salt and pepper

2 ounces (¼ cup) extra-virgin olive oil

1 pinch fresh rosemary, chopped

1 pinch fresh thyme leaves

FOR THE
BABY GREENS

4 small handfuls assorted baby lettuces, rinsed (frisée, lolla rossa, mizuna, etc.)

4 whole chives

Extra-virgin olive oil, for drizzling over lettuces

Sherry vinegar, for sprinkling lightly over lettuces

Salt and pepper

FOR THE RED PEPPER SYRUP

- Place red pepper juice in a small sauce pot and reduce over high heat to about 3 ounces (6 tablespoons.)
- Let cool, then add the vinegar. Add sugar, salt, and pepper to taste.
- Serve at room temperature. Can be prepared up to two days ahead and refrigerated.

FOR THE LAMB

- Preheat the oven to 275°F.
- Season the lamb loins with salt and pepper.
- Place the olive oil in an ovenproof sauté pan, add the lamb, and gently brown over medium heat, 1 minute per side. Do not allow the lamb to sear or get too brown.
- Add rosemary and thyme and baste the meat with the pan juices.
- Transfer to the oven and roast, turning the meat over and basting every 5 minutes, until medium-rare, about 18 minutes.
- Allow the meat to rest about 10 minutes when it is finished; it will be served just warm.

FOR THE BABY LETTUCE BOUQUETS

- Divide the lettuce into four bunches (just as you would a bouquet of flowers).
- Wrap a chive strand a few times around the base of each bunch to hold the lettuces together and tie it off.

TO SERVE

- For each plate, form two quenelles of the eggplant salad, placing them like spokes on a wheel at 8 and 10 o'clock.
- Slice each lamb loin into six even pieces. Arrange three slices on each plate, fanning them out to extend from 1 to 4 o'clock.
- Place the lettuce bouquets between the eggplant and the lamb and drizzle with oil and vinegar.
- Drizzle Red Pepper Syrup in a circle around the eggplant and lamb. Garnish with freshly ground pepper and a drizzle of olive oil and serve.

MISINFORMED YOUTH When I first started in the restaurant business, the only chefs who received any real respect were European. This led me to some pretty crazy notions about how to attain success. For example, could you ever become a great chef if you did not have a fantastic-sounding French name, like Jean-Louis or Jean-Claude or Jean-whatever? Forget about a television show, fame, or a best-selling cookbook — who's going to spend hard-earned money on a meal made by a guy named Michael Schlow? If only I had a better name. . . .

Maybe I should change it. Would the meal somehow have more appeal if it was created by a fictional French character? If so, what would I name him? Maybe Jean-Charles Loupe de Mer would do the trick. I would have been impressed with his cooking by name alone! His escargot would have been a real crowd pleaser, the stuff they write folk songs about. And his soufflés? Downright dreamy. With Jean-Charles manning the stoves, the guests would've busted down the door, just trying to get a taste of perfection.

Fortunately, a simple reality check and a change in the restaurant landscape here in America wiped all those ridiculous thoughts away. As a young cook, I began to hear and read about chefs such as Jasper White, Jeremiah Tower, Mark Miller, Alice Waters, Norman Van Aiken, and Larry Forgione — American chefs who were influenced by their past experiences and by the area of the country in which they lived. A new generation of chefs was coming of age, and they were creating modern, regional styles of American cooking. They were more serious and more respected, and they were practicing their craft right here under our noses. Not only was the playing field changing, it was getting a whole lot bigger. It started to sound like there was hope for me after all, and maybe I could even keep my name.

MAINE CRAB TART

WITH CUCUMBER, CILANTRO, AND BROKEN CUMIN VINAIGRETTE

This makes an impressive first course, and it is surprisingly simple to prepare. You can make the Broken Cumin Vinaigrette a day ahead, but the rest of the dish should be done within three hours of serving or the flavors become diluted and the crab mixture will need reseasoning. Extra vinaigrette can be refrigerated for several days and tossed with mixed greens.

NOTE If you do not own ring molds, no worries. You can make your own, either by cutting the bottom out of a paper cup, or — and this yields even better results — by removing the top and bottom lids from a 6-ounce tuna can the next time you make sandwiches. Peel away the label, wash the can thoroughly, and you will be the proud owner of your first ring mold. Keep feeding your family tuna sandwiches and you'll have a full set in no time. For this recipe, you will need two molds.

TRUC For a polished, professional-looking presentation, spoon the vinaigrette around the tarts by letting it drizzle off the tip of the spoon rather than the side. You should see little droplets of the vinegar floating in the oil when you spoon the vinaigrette onto the plate.

Makes 2 first courses

FOR THE TARTS

- Combine the crab, mayonnaise, thyme, chives, shallot, lemon juice, and 2 tablespoons olive oil in a small mixing bowl.
- Season the crab mixture with salt, pepper, and a pinch or two of sugar.
- In a second bowl, toss the cucumbers with the rice wine vinegar and salt, to taste.
- Refrigerate both bowls until ready to serve.

FOR THE BROKEN CUMIN VINAIGRETTE

- Simmer the balsamic vinegar in a small saucepan until reduced to 2 ounces (¼ cup).
- Place cumin seeds in a small sauté pan and toast over high heat until lightly browned and fragrant, about 2 minutes.
- Coarsely crack the cumin seeds using a mortar and pestle or spice grinder. (Or place them on a cutting board, cover them with the bottom of a sauce pan, and crush them by pressing down firmly.)
- Combine the vinegar, cumin seeds, and the remaining ingredients in a small bowl, whisking only a few times to incorporate. The vinaigrette should not be smooth and emulsified, but "broken" with visible droplets of vinegar suspended in the oil.

FOR THE TARTS

- 6 ounces jumbo lump crabmeat, picked clean of any cartilage
- 1 tablespoon mayonnaise
- 1 pinch fresh thyme, chopped
- 1 teaspoon thinly sliced chives
- 1 tablespoon chopped shallots
- Juice of half a lemon
- 1 ounce (2 tablespoons) extra-virgin olive oil, plus additional for oiling the molds
- Salt and pepper, to taste
- Sugar
- 4 tablespoons English cucumber, peeled and cut into perfect ¼-inch dice
- ½ ounce (1 tablespoon) rice wine vinegar
- 2 pinches micro-cilantro, for garnish (available from specialty grocers; regular cilantro, chopped, can be substituted)

FOR THE BROKEN CUMIN VINAIGRETTE

- 7 ounces (¾ cup plus 2 tablespoons) balsamic vinegar
- ½ teaspoon cumin seeds
- 4 ounces (½ cup) canola oil
- 1 tablespoon minced shallots
- 1 teaspoon chives, finely sliced
- 1 small pinch curry powder
- Salt and pepper, to taste

directions are continued on following page

TO SERVE

- At serving time, check both the crab and cucumber mixtures for seasoning and adjust if needed.
- Lightly brush the inside of two 2½ x 1½-inch ring molds with olive oil.
- Drain the cucumbers of any excess liquid.
- Put each ring mold in the center of a dinner plate.
- Place 2 tablespoons of the cucumber mixture in each ring mold.
- Spoon half the crabmeat over the cucumbers in each mold and press down gently.
- Carefully remove the molds.
- Spoon a teaspoon of the vinaigrette around each tart, being careful to leave the vinaigrette "broken" by not stirring too much.
- Garnish tarts with a few micro-cilantro leaves and serve.

POTATO-CRUSTED HALIBUT
WITH WILD MUSHROOMS AND HARICOTS VERTS, TRUFFLE VINAIGRETTE, AND CARROT REDUCTION

Are you ever going to look good making this one. Your guests will be so impressed they won't know what hit them. Be prepared for someone to cry foul and accuse you of bringing in a ringer for the dinner. Actually, preparing this halibut is not as difficult as it might seem at first glance. So read through the recipe closely — read it twice, just to be sure — and have everything ready before you start cooking.

NOTE Before turning your attention to the halibut, prepare the Truffle Vinaigrette and the Carrot Reduction; they can be made several days ahead, but bring them to room temperature before serving. When you are ready to cook, start with the wild mushrooms and haricots verts, lower the heat when they are almost finished, and then start in on the halibut.

ANOTHER NOTE Any leftover Truffle Vinaigrette or Carrot Reduction can be used to garnish the Loin of Venison with Lentils and Celery Root Puree (page 182).

Makes 4 main courses

FOR THE WILD MUSHROOMS AND HARICOTS VERTS
- Melt the olive oil and butter in a sauté pan over high heat.
- Add the shallot and cook for 1 minute.
- Add the mushrooms, season with salt and pepper, and sauté for 3 minutes.
- Reduce the heat to medium, add the blanched haricots verts, and sauté for 1 minute more.
- Add the thyme leaves and reduce the heat to low while you prepare the halibut.
- Just before serving, drizzle the lemon juice over the vegetables, taste, and adjust seasoning.

FOR THE HALIBUT
- Beat the egg yolks with salt and pepper in a shallow pan (a pie pan works great) to make an egg wash.
- Combine the potato flakes with the thyme leaves and spread out on a plate or shallow pan.
- Season the fillets with salt and pepper on one side only.
- Dip just the seasoned side of the fish into the egg wash, being careful not to let any egg wash drip down the sides of the fish.
- Dip the egg-washed side of the fish into the seasoned potato flakes and press down a bit to make them adhere. Set aside, crust-side down.
- Repeat with the remaining fillets.
- Pour the olive oil into a large sauté pan, arrange the fillets crust-side down

directions are continued on following page

FOR THE WILD MUSHROOMS AND HARICOTS VERTS

1 ounce (2 tablespoons) canola oil

1 tablespoon butter

1 large shallot, sliced into thin rings

2 cups cleaned and sliced assorted wild mushrooms (use whatever looks best at the market)

1 cup haricots verts, blanched 1 minute in salted, boiling water, then plunged into ice water, drained, and cut in half

1 pinch fresh thyme leaves, chopped

Juice of half a lemon

FOR THE POTATO-CRUSTED HALIBUT

2 egg yolks

Salt and pepper

1 cup all-natural dehydrated potato flakes

1 pinch fresh thyme leaves, chopped

4 6-ounce halibut fillets, skins removed

3 ounces (6 tablespoons) pure olive oil

Juice of half a lemon

1 ounce (2 tablespoons) Carrot Reduction (recipe follows)

1 ounce (2 tablespoons) Truffle Vinaigrette (recipe follows)

in the pan, and place on the burner over medium-high heat. (That's right: do not preheat the sauté pan; I promise the fish will not stick!)

- After about 3 minutes, the crust should be golden brown, if it is not, raise the heat to high and continue cooking.
- When the crust has turned golden brown, season the fish with salt and pepper, flip it over, and cook for 1 minute.
- Remove from heat, and leave the fillets in the pan for 1 minute.
- Deglaze the pan with the lemon juice, being careful not to squeeze it directly on the fish, which would soften the crisp crust you have worked so hard to develop. Swirl the pan a few times to incorporate the lemon juice.

TO SERVE

- Spoon the Wild Mushrooms and Haricots Verts into the center of four dinner plates.
- Arrange the halibut, crust-side up, on top of the vegetables.
- Spoon a few drops of Carrot Reduction (it should be at room temperature) around the edge of the plate.
- Spoon some Truffle Vinaigrette around the Carrot Reduction, and serve.

CARROT REDUCTION

Makes 6 tablespoons, enough for 4 courses of Potato-Crusted Halibut

8 ounces (1 cup) carrot juice (use your juicer)

A few drops extra-virgin olive oil, if needed

1 pinch curry powder

Salt, to taste

Sugar, to taste

2 tablespoons rice wine vinegar

- Reduce the carrot juice to 4 tablespoons over high heat.
- If the juice separates, don't panic, just keep reducing it. When you are down to 4 tablespoons, add a few drops of olive oil and whisk vigorously to bring it back together.
- Add the remaining ingredients and whisk to incorporate.
- This reduction can be frozen, or will keep in the refrigerator for up to two weeks.

TRUFFLE VINAIGRETTE

Makes 10 tablespoons, enough for 4 courses of Potato-Crusted Halibut

3½ ounces (7 tablespoons) balsamic vinegar

1 shallot, minced

1 pinch fresh thyme leaves, chopped

4 ounces (8 tablespoons) truffle oil

½ teaspoon finely sliced chives

Salt and pepper, to taste

- Boil balsamic vinegar in a small saucepot until reduced to 2 tablespoons.
- Transfer the reduced vinegar to a small bowl and add the remaining ingredients, whisking just until combined. (The oil and vinegar will separate over time; no need to worry!) This vinaigrette can be stored in the refrigerator up to four days.

SEARED TUNA "NICOISE-STYLE"

WITH SPICY LEMON VINAIGRETTE AND ENGLISH CUCUMBER SALAD

The traditional Tuna Salad Nicoise has become a tired staple at American garden-club luncheons. This modern version replaces the can of Starkist or Chicken of the Sea with fresh, sushi-grade tuna and uses a simple Spicy Lemon Vinaigrette instead of bottled dressing. I removed the usual potatoes and added crisp English cucumbers to create a fresh, vibrant salad.

NOTE It's okay to cook the tuna up to two hours before you want to serve it. Slice it as soon as it comes out of the pan, which allows it to retain that beautiful red interior, then cover it with plastic and store it in the fridge until serving time.

Makes lunch for 4

- Remove the tomatoes from the oil and chop, draining any excess liquid.
- Combine the tomatoes, 1 teaspoon minced shallot, chopped parsley, and 1 pinch thyme. Season with salt and pepper and reserve.
- Arrange the cucumbers in two rows of 4 to 5 slices each down the center of each plate. Season with salt and a few drops of the lemon juice.
- Combine the haricots verts with the shallot rings, chopped egg, and 2 tablespoons of Spicy Lemon Vinaigrette. Season with salt and pepper and toss together gently.
- Spread the haricots verts mixture along the top of the cucumber slices.
- Place fennel seeds in a small sauté pan and toast over high heat until lightly browned and fragrant, about 2 minutes.
- Coarsely crack the fennel seeds using a mortar and pestle or spice grinder. (Or place them on a cutting board, cover them with the bottom of a sauce pan, and crush them by pressing down firmly.)
- Place a dry sauté pan over high heat for 2 to 3 minutes, until very hot.
- Add the canola oil and swirl around the pan.
- Rub both sides of the tuna pieces with fennel seeds, the remaining 2 pinches thyme, and salt and pepper.
- When the oil in the pan is very hot, sear the tuna for 30 seconds to 1 minute on each side.
- Deglaze with the remaining lemon juice and remove the tuna pieces from the pan, transferring them to a cutting board.
- Immediately cut each piece into five slices with a sharp knife and arrange in a line over the haricots verts.
- Spoon 1 tablespoon of Tomato Confit mixture down the center of the tuna.
- Drizzle 1 tablespoon of Spicy Lemon Vinaigrette over and around the tuna on each plate, and serve.

4 tablespoons chopped Tomato Confit (page 185)

1 shallot, sliced into thin rings (mince some of these rings so that you have 1 teaspoon minced shallot)

1 tablespoon chopped Italian parsley

3 pinches fresh thyme leaves, chopped

Salt and pepper

1 English cucumber, sliced into ⅓-inch-thick rounds (you will need 8 to 10 rounds per plate)

Juice of 1 lemon

1½ cups haricots verts, blanched and cut in half

1 hard-boiled egg, chopped

3 ounces (6 tablespoons) Spicy Lemon Vinaigrette (page 219)

½ teaspoon fennel seeds

2 ounces (¼ cup) canola oil

4 5-ounce pieces #1 grade sushi-quality tuna (ask the fish guy for pieces that are 4 inches long, 3 inches wide, and 2 inches thick)

WARNING! READ CLOSELY! From time to time, guests come in and tell me how they went to this or that particular restaurant, and the chef there had been so incredibly creative. Since I'm a glutton for punishment, I always take the bait. "What did you have?" I inquire.

"Well," they start, "he took this piece of tilapia and dipped it in some miso-chipotle-tarragon panko crumbs. He cooked the fish in curry oil until it was nice and crispy. Then he placed the fish on a bed of vegetables, I think there was jicama, arugula, snap peas, edamame beans, taro root, and something else . . . that was on top of the jasmine rice cake with sesame seeds. The sauce was where he really showed his artistic prowess; there were two, actually, intertwined. One was a cumin–thai chile buerre monte, and the other was truffle vinaigrette. Oh, and he topped the whole thing with some crispy fried leeks for a garnish."

Uh huh. I had to ask. . . .

Very early in my career I suffered from a similar affliction, although maybe my case was not quite so extreme. I refer to it as Kitchen Sink Syndrome, KSS. You who suffer from this know who you are. You add way too many ingredients to every dish, and you may even make the occasional diner ill through your "experimentation." Omelets loaded with tons of cheese, lots of deli meats, assorted vegetables, and hot sauce were my "signature" back then. And I was particularly fond of some vague dried spice concoction called "Italian seasonings" that matured in our cupboard for God knows how long. Don't ask, but I put it in everything.

Luckily, there is a cure for KSS. It's called restraint and simplicity.

I am forever encouraging my cooks to be creative, but keep it simple. For some reason, people seem to think creative cooking is synonymous with complicated cooking. If it's simple, then it's merely plain. I shake my head at this line of reasoning.

Once you've managed to procure the best products available, the real challenge is to cook them correctly and let their flavors speak for themselves. It is far more important to focus on the quality of your products and the techniques you use than it is to worry about a laundry list of ingredients that only muddles the final results. Combining ingredients for a dish is like devising a scene for a movie. It's best to highlight one flavor or ingredient, and let it have the meal's starring role. Surround this budding starlet with a supporting cast of just two or three background flavors that complement, rather than steal the show. Follow my lead, and I promise your KSS symptoms will disappear before you know it.

LOIN OF VENISON
WITH LENTILS AND CELERY ROOT PUREE

FOR THE CELERY ROOT PUREE

2 large celery roots, peeled and cut into 2-inch cubes

About 1 quart whole milk, enough to cover the celery root in a small pot

2 tablespoons butter

4 tablespoons extra-virgin olive oil

Salt and white pepper

Sugar

Juice of one lemon

FOR THE LENTILS

1 teaspoon bacon fat (optional)

1 teaspoon butter

1 shallot, minced

1 cup cooked black or French green lentils (about ½ cup uncooked)

1 teaspoon sherry vinegar

1 pinch fresh rosemary, chopped

Salt and pepper

If you think venison is too challenging for a home cook, you're in for a surprise; it's probably harder to grill a good burger or make a perfect dish of pasta. The only ironclad rule is that venison should be served rare to medium-rare. Cooked any further and it tends to take on a livery, cardboard taste. And since venison is low in fat, it does not need to rest after cooking like other meats. The rest of the menu is a breeze to put together. Both the celery root puree and the lentils are simple yet elegant dishes that pair beautifully with the venison or with other roasted meats. To further highlight the rich, earthy flavors of the venison, you can serve this dish with Truffle Vinaigrette or the Carrot Reduction from page 176.

NOTE: You can make the lentils and celery root puree a day in advance and reheat them just before serving. That way, the only thing that requires your attention at the last minute is the venison.

ANOTHER NOTE To cook lentils, soak several hours or overnight in cold water. Drain, then place in a pot with plenty of lightly salted water and bring to a boil. Reduce heat and simmer until tender, 25 to 45 minutes, depending on the variety.

Makes dinner for 4

FOR THE CELERY ROOT PUREE
- Place the celery root in a sauce pot, cover with milk, and set over medium heat.
- Cook until the celery root is very tender but not mushy, adjusting the heat if needed to maintain a steady simmer.
- Strain, reserving the milk.
- Transfer the celery root to a food processor and process until it starts to break up.
- Add the butter and olive oil and puree until smooth.
- If the puree seems too stiff, continue processing and add some of the reserved milk, a few ounces at a time, until creamy.
- Season with salt and white pepper. Add sugar (a pinch at a time, to taste) and the lemon juice.
- Taste and adjust seasoning, if necessary. Reheat gently before serving.

FOR THE LENTILS
- Heat the bacon fat (if using) and the butter in a small pan over high heat.
- Add the shallot and cook for 2 minutes.
- Add the lentils and cook for 2 minutes to reheat.
- Stir in the vinegar and rosemary, and season with salt and pepper.
- Adjust seasoning if needed. If made in advance, reheat gently before serving.

FOR THE VENISON

- Preheat the oven to 300°F.
- Heat the olive oil over moderate heat in an ovenproof sauté pan.
- Season the venison with salt and pepper.
- When the oil is hot, sauté the venison for 1 minute per side, adjusting heat if needed to keep it from browning.
- Add the rosemary, thyme, and butter to the pan, swirl to combine, and cook another minute, basting the venison with the pan juices several times with a large spoon.
- Place venison in the oven and roast 10 to 12 minutes for rare to medium-rare, basting every 2 to 3 minutes with the pan juices.

TO SERVE

- Spoon one-quarter of the celery root puree into the middle of each of four dinner plates.
- Using the back of a small ladle (a 2-ounce ladle is perfect), spin out the celery root puree into a 6-inch circle; that is, spread out the puree using a circular motion, as if you were spreading tomato sauce on a pizza.
- Spoon ¼ cup lentils into the center of each circle of puree.
- Arrange the venison on top of the lentils.
- Spoon Truffle Vinaigrette or Carrot Reduction, a teaspoon or so, around the circle of celery root puree, if desired, and serve.

FOR THE
VENISON

2 ounces (¼ cup) pure olive oil

4 7-ounce venison loins

Salt and pepper

1 pinch fresh
rosemary, chopped

1 pinch fresh thyme
leaves, chopped

2 tablespoons butter

ORZO GRATIN
WITH BLACK OLIVES, TOMATO CONFIT, AND GOAT CHEESE

1 pound orzo, uncooked

½ ounce (1 tablespoon) extra-virgin olive oil

2 tablespoons butter

1 shallot, minced

3 cups milk

2 cups heavy cream

4 ounces goat cheese, crumbled

¼ cup grated Parmigiano-Reggiano cheese

16 to 18 black olives (Gaeta or Kalamata), rinsed in cold water, pitted, and quartered

4 tablespoons roughly chopped Tomato Confit (recipe follows)

2 large pinches fresh thyme leaves, chopped

Salt, pepper, and crushed red pepper flakes, to taste

Crunchy Bread-Crumb Topping (recipe follows)

For the ultimate professional flourish, present this gratin to your guests in individual serving dishes. I use tiny copper pots at the restaurant, but ramekins or custard cups will also work. Of course, you can also bring this to the table in a regular casserole dish, but everybody seems to fight over the crunchy stuff on top. With individual serving dishes, nobody has to share.

NOTE Like lasagna, this is one of those dishes that can be made a day or so in advance and then reheated. It actually tastes better that way. If you do prepare it ahead of time, cook the orzo mixture only 10 to 15 minutes. Remove from heat, let cool, and then refrigerate. Reheat gently before adding the topping and finishing under the broiler. If the orzo seems to have absorbed too much liquid after cooling, you may have to add a few more ounces of milk before reheating.

ANOTHER NOTE The Crunchy Bread-Crumb Topping can also be made ahead and stored in the refrigerator.

Makes 6 side dishes, excellent with roast chicken or lamb

- Cook orzo in salted, boiling water until al dente. Drain, toss with olive oil, and set aside.
- Melt the butter in a large saucepan over medium heat.
- Add the minced shallot and cook for 2 minutes.
- Stir in the milk, cream, and cheeses.
- Add the orzo, olives, Tomato Confit, thyme, salt, pepper, and crushed red pepper flakes.
- Cook for 10 to 15 minutes, stirring occasionally, until the mixture becomes rich and creamy.
- Set aside for 30 minutes to allow orzo to absorb most of the liquid. (The orzo mixture can be prepared to this point and then refrigerated overnight.)
- Transfer orzo mixture to a casserole or baking dish, or to six individual ovenproof serving dishes. (If you've prepared the orzo mixture ahead, gently reheat before assembling the dish. If needed, add a few tablespoons of milk to the orzo while reheating.)
- Sprinkle Crunchy Bread-Crumb Topping over the orzo mixture and place under a preheated broiler until golden brown. (If you have one of those propane torches for making crème brûlée, here's another opportunity to use it.)
- Serve.

TOMATO CONFIT

(OLIVE OIL–POACHED TOMATOES)

When you can't find really ripe tomatoes, this is the way to go. It's not cheating — really, it's not. All you're doing is coaxing a little extra flavor out of a precious fruit when it's not quite at its prime. Use these tomatoes to top bruschetta, or finely chop and serve along with their flavorful oil on grilled fish or chicken.

8 plum tomatoes, halved lengthwise

Pure olive oil, enough to cover the tomatoes

1 clove garlic, halved

1 sprig thyme

Salt and pepper

1 pinch of sugar

Makes 8 poached tomatoes

- Preheat the oven to 225°F.
- Sprinkle the cut-sides of the tomatoes with a pinch of salt, pepper, and sugar.
- Allow to sit for 10 minutes.
- Transfer the tomatoes to an ovenproof pan or casserole dish large enough to hold them. They do not have to be arranged in a single layer.
- Pour enough oil over the tomatoes to cover them completely.
- Add the garlic and thyme sprig to the oil.
- Bake the tomatoes in the oven, uncovered, for 45 minutes to 1 hour. When done, the tomatoes will be tender and their skins will be wrinkled. Check the pot occasionally to make sure the oil does not boil.
- Remove from oven and let cool completely.
- You can store the tomatoes, submerged in the oil, for up to two weeks in the fridge.

CRUNCHY BREAD-CRUMB TOPPING

Makes enough to cover 6 servings of Orzo Gratin

- Mix everything in a bowl and make sure the butter is well incorporated.

1 cup bread crumbs (preferably panko)

1 pinch fresh thyme leaves, chopped

1 pinch fresh rosemary, chopped

½ cup grated Parmigiano-Reggiano cheese

1 tablespoon butter, soft

JAPANESE NOODLE SOUP
WITH SHELLFISH AND VEGETABLES

4 cups dashi broth

2 ounces (¼ cup) rice
wine vinegar

2 ounces (¼ cup) mirin
(Japanese rice wine)

1 ounce (2 tablespoons) light
soy sauce

¼ teaspoon togarashi (see note
on page 24; cayenne pepper
can be substituted)

20 bite-size broccoli florets

1 small carrot, peeled and
sliced into thin rounds

½ white onion, sliced thinly

1 pound fresh Japanese soba or
rice noodles

1 cup snap peas, trimmed

3-inch piece lotus root, cut
into 12 thin slices

16 medium shrimp, shelled,
deveined, and halved
lengthwise

8 large sea scallops, halved

½ cup whole cilantro leaves

½ cup whole Thai basil leaves

10 mint leaves

4 tablespoons thinly sliced
scallions, for garnish

Prepare this soup and your guests will be impressed to discover your repertoire extends to Japanese cuisine. They'll also wonder how in the world you ever found the time to hone your skills. To demonstrate just how well you've mastered Japanese culture and to make the dinner truly authentic, serve this with chopsticks, miso-soup spoons, and a small container of togarashi. And be sure to encourage everyone to slurp the noodle soup really loud, just like you were shown by your *sensei* in Yokahama.

NOTE The distinctive background flavors of this soup come from dashi broth, the classic Japanese soup base made from dried bonito flakes. Purists might insist on making the broth from scratch instead of from a packaged soup base, but I think in this soup instant dashi is fine — even traditional Japanese cooks use it in their cooking. It comes in both powdered and liquid forms, and either one can be used — just follow the directions on the label.

Makes dinner for 4

- Bring the dashi broth, rice wine vinegar, mirin, soy sauce, and togarashi to boil in a large soup pot over high heat.
- Reduce heat and simmer for 10 minutes to allow the flavors to marry.
- Add the broccoli, carrot, and onion to the soup and cook for 2 minutes.
- Turn up the heat to high and bring the soup to a boil. Add the noodles and boil for about 2 minutes.
- Add the snap peas, lotus root, shrimp, and scallops and cook for 3 minutes, until the seafood is gently cooked.
- Remove the pot from heat, add the cilantro, Thai basil, and mint, and steep for 1 minute.
- Divide the soup between four large bowls, garnish with thinly sliced scallions, and serve.

RED WINE-POACHED PEARS

WITH ST. AGUR CHEESE AND HAZELNUTS

Slightly sweet, spicy, and aromatic, these poached pears are an extraordinary way to end a meal. They are easy to put together, and you can eat them with little or no guilt. If you cannot find St. Agur cheese, substitute Gorgonzola, Papillon Roquefort, or any other soft, creamy blue cheese.

Serves 2

- Combine the red wine, water, orange juice, sugar, vanilla bean, cloves, and peppercorns in a medium sauce pot and place over medium heat.
- Add the pears and simmer slowly until just tender when pierced with a toothpick or small knife; the exact timing will depend on ripeness of the pears. Remove the pears from the liquid and set aside to cool.
- Place chopped nuts in a small sauté pan and toast over high heat until lightly browned and fragrant, about 2 minutes.
- Strain the poaching liquid. Return it to the sauce pot and cook over medium-high heat until reduced to a light syrup.
- Meanwhile, divide the cheese into four parts and roll each piece into a small ball. Keep in a cool place. (This can be done up to an hour before dinner.)
- Cut each pear in half and place on dessert plates.
- Arrange two balls of cheese on each plate and pour a few spoonfuls of syrup around the pears.
- Sprinkle hazelnuts over the pears and serve.

2 cups good-quality red cooking wine

8 ounces (1 cup) water

2 ounces (¼ cup) orange juice

1 cup sugar

1 vanilla bean

4 cloves

6 black peppercorns

2 slightly firm Bosc pears, peeled, cored, and left whole (leave stem on for presentation)

4 ounces St. Agur blue cheese

¼ cup chopped hazelnuts

Chapter 8

TIME TO CELEBRATE

THE SEASONS, LIFE,
FOR NO SPECIAL REASON AT ALL

Maybe you've tried at least a couple of the recipes in this book. You've gained some skill and confidence, and the recipes worked. (They did work, didn't they?) The next thing on the agenda is to throw a little party, and guess what — you're cooking for it! It's only natural for you to want to show off your cooking prowess for friends and family. And here's my promise: Not only are you going to make some pretty special food, you're even going to love doing it. Some of this stuff may seem a bit more complicated, but I'm here to spot you.

This chapter features two set menus — a festive winter gathering for dinner and a springtime luncheon. Why only two and why these two? I like to think of my choices as arbitrary but not clichéd. The cold-weather feast could be for an intimate group of friends before the onslaught of holiday parties and other events. The occasion for the spring luncheon could be graduation, Mother's Day, or for no special reason at all. As far as the set menus go, all recipes are written for tasting-size portions, and some can even be used as appetizers when paired with dishes from other chapters.

Although we see tasting menus all over America these days, the "degustation" was not at all common as recently as twenty-five years ago. For his role in helping to popularize it, I would like to pay homage to Jean-Louis Palladin. Palladin may not have been the first or only chef to create tasting menus, but he was certainly ahead of his time in this country. Before coming to the United States from France, Jean-Louis, age 26, was the youngest chef to ever receive two Michelin stars. And then he went on to simply work magic at his eponymous restaurant in Washington, D.C.; some of the best chefs in America today spent time there. The cost of ingredients never came into play for him. It was the experience — friends, food, and surroundings — that mattered. The composition and cadence of his menus merged cooking with performance art. He understood what entertaining and hospitality were all about.

So while we're cooking celebratory meals, I would also like to dedicate this chapter to celebrating Palladin's life. He passed away far too early, in fall 2001 at the age of 54. The culinary world is lucky to have had him, even if for such a short time. If Jean-Louis were here today, you can bet he'd want to create a menu with caviar, lobster, foie gras, and champagne — celebrating his memory gives me the perfect excuse to have one over-the-top chapter in my book!

With Jean-Louis's commitment to a good time in mind, let's start with an early step in the process that people too often regard as merely a chore to get past: shopping. Sometimes good shopping doesn't mean hunting down a bargain. Sometimes it means spending a little money. Good shopping, however, mostly means thinking things through and making the extra effort. In the old days, my grandmother would go all over New York City to buy her ingredients: specialty bread in one place, fresh fish in another, dairy someplace else, pristine vegetables in another. Many towns in America still allow you to do this — you just might have to drive a mile in a different direction. Still, it's possible, and certainly not unreasonable. I never really understood how people will spend six hours in the kitchen cooking for a special meal, but look at you like you're crazy if you suggest they stop at one more store for, say, the perfect brioche to round out the meal.

As a chef, I have access to incredible products delivered overnight to my restaurants. But I have to be just as savvy as anybody else when cooking at home. I've come to realize a lot of shopping is about asking: Ask to smell the fish, rather than just watch it get wrapped up and taking it, then returning home to find it reeks of that strong odor that fish you're about to eat really should not have. If you call ahead, ask if the butcher can order you hanger steak. Does the guy in the vegetable section have any better-looking herbs? Ask.

The concept of seasonality in cooking is something many cookbooks mention, and it really is important. Spring is easy. Produce markets overflow with fresh fava beans, peas, morels, ramps — items that let you know warm weather is just around the corner.

Winter is a different story. Although the calendar divides the year into just four seasons, in Boston, where I live, the weather varies so often it feels more like ten, most of them cold. And since winter in one form or another is a factor for most of us, why not make the best of it? To celebrate both winter and spring in style, I've devised recipes that feature some of the delicacies of both seasons, and dishes that are so good the celebrations might become annual traditions.

WINTER

What fun,
it may change into snow —
the winter rain
Basho

WINTER TASTING MENU

Soft Scrambled Eggs with Caviar
Chilled Lobster Salad with Citrus and Fennel
Seared Foie Gras with Mango and Mango Vinaigrette
Loin of Veal with Black Trumpet Mushroom Ragout
Chocolate Cinnamon Bonets Infused with Bay Leaf

SOFT SCRAMBLED EGGS
WITH CAVIAR

Taking care of fellow members of the restaurant business always gives me pleasure. Since restaurant people provide hospitality all day long, it's a bona fide treat to take care of them for a change. When my good friend Joe Bastianich came to dinner at Radius one winter night, I wanted to celebrate his visit with great fanfare. Joe is a big-time New York City restaurateur, and I wanted to show him excellent food could be found in Boston as well. When I presented him with this dish to start the meal, he gave me a puzzled look and said, "Caviar and scrambled eggs? That's a new one on me."

These were perfectly cooked scrambled eggs, creamy and warm, combined with slightly salty, cool Osetra caviar. Joe devoured them, gave me a wink and an approving nod, and we moved on to the next course. After the meal, he told me he had enjoyed everything, each course was right on, just great. "But what you did to those eggs, *that* was definitely out of this world."

TRUC To make perfect toast points, sauté thin bread slices in a little bit of butter in a nonstick pan over medium-high heat. Cook until golden, but don't let them get too brittle.

NOTE Teacups make attractive serving dishes for the eggs.

Makes 4 first courses

8 large eggs

2 ounces (¼ cup) heavy cream

1 teaspoon butter

Salt and black pepper

1 tablespoon sliced chives

2 ounces Osetra caviar (Beluga would be a decadent choice, too)

8 triangles of toasted brioche (or any soft bread)

- Whisk the eggs in a mixing bowl until light and frothy, about 2 minutes.
- Whisk in the cream.
- Heat a nonstick pan over medium heat and melt the butter.
- Pour in the eggs, reduce the heat to low, and cook very slowly, folding the eggs over with a spatula every 30 seconds or so.
- After the eggs start to bind, season with salt and pepper.
- As the eggs begin to set, add the chives.
- Check the seasoning and remove from the heat as soon as the eggs are a creamy pale yellow and softly scrambled.
- Spoon the eggs into four serving cups.
- Garnish each egg cup with ½ ounce caviar and accompany with two toast points.
- Serve immediately, while still warm!

CHILLED LOBSTER SALAD
WITH CITRUS AND FENNEL

2 1-pound lobsters, cooked for 6 minutes in boiling water, plunged into ice water, and then removed from their shells

1½ cups Fennel-Grapefruit Broth (recipe follows)

1 large bulb fennel, halved

1 ruby red grapefruit cut into 8 segments, cleaned of zest and pith

8 to 10 tarragon leaves, roughly chopped

You might not know it, but the fish guy at most supermarkets will cook and shell your lobsters for you while you wait. Be sure you give clear instructions about cooking times, and remember, lobsters aren't Minute Rice — they can be over- or undercooked. One-pound lobsters should be boiled for about 6 minutes, but the counter people at my supermarket tend to want to cook them a lot longer for some unknown reason. Or maybe they just get caught up helping all the other customers and forget about me and my poor lobsters.

NOTE The broth can be made up to a day in advance, and the fennel can be sliced several hours ahead of time and kept in a bowl of cold water.

TRUC To cut beautiful-looking fennel slices, hold the vegetable upright and cut it in half lengthwise. Slicing from the core- to the stem-end and working from the cut-side outward, shave the fennel into thin pieces. (A mandoline makes easy work out of this, otherwise a super-sharp knife is essential.) The resulting slices will look like an opened hand.

Makes 4 first courses

- Slice the lobster tails lengthwise into halves.
- Brush 2 ounces (4 tablespoons) of Fennel-Grapefruit Broth on the lobster tails and claws and refrigerate 3 to 5 minutes while you prepare the fennel.
- Using a mandoline or very sharp knife, shave the fennel lengthwise into very thin sheets.
- Combine the shaved fennel, grapefruit segments, tarragon, and 2 more ounces (4 tablespoons) Fennel-Grapefruit Broth in a mixing bowl and set aside for 2 minutes to let the flavors blend.
- Remove the lobster from the refrigerator, drain any liquid that has accumulated, and divide between four bowls, placing one halved lobster tail and one claw in each bowl.
- Drain any excess liquid from the fennel mixture. Divide the fennel between the four bowls, mounding it on top of the lobster.
- Divide the remaining Fennel-Grapefruit Broth between the bowls, ladling it carefully around the lobster.

FENNEL-GRAPEFRUIT BROTH

Makes 1½ cups, enough for 4 servings of Chilled Lobster Salad

- Bring the grapefruit juice and Pernod to a boil in a small sauce pot and reduce over high heat to just over 1½ cups.
- Meanwhile, toast the fennel seeds in a nonstick pan over high heat for 2 minutes. Let cool. Add cooled fennel seeds and the remaining ingredients to the grapefruit broth and steep for 30 minutes.
- Strain and refrigerate.
- Can be made 1 day in advance.

3 cups grapefruit juice

2 ounces (¼ cup) Pernod

2 teaspoons fennel seeds

2 tablespoons chopped shallots

1 teaspoon sugar

½ teaspoon chopped fresh tarragon

1 tablespoon rice wine vinegar

SEARED FOIE GRAS

WITH MANGO AND MANGO VINAIGRETTE

12 ounces foie gras, trimmed of any veins or discolored spots

1 ripe mango, peeled, pitted, and cut into small dice

1 tablespoon minced shallot

1 pinch fresh thyme, chopped

1 pinch sugar

½ ounce (1 tablespoon) rice wine vinegar

½ ounce (1 tablespoon) extra-virgin olive oil

1 teaspoon finely sliced chives

Salt and pepper

2 tablespoons toasted hazelnuts, crushed

4 teaspoons Mango Vinaigrette (recipe follows)

If you have never cooked foie gras at home, don't be intimidated. Just follow these instructions, and I promise you success. Good accompaniments to foie gras tend to have sweet and slightly tart components to counterbalance the richness of the liver. Fruit always seem to go well, but don't limit yourself to the obvious apples and pears. I once put Foie Gras with Caramelized Macomber Turnips and Sweet and Sour Beet Vinaigrette on the menu at Radius, and the combination worked beautifully.

TRUC Let foie gras come to room temperature before sautéing it, and do not preheat the pan. When foie gras comes straight from the fridge it is almost like chilled butter. Now, if you tried to sauté a stick of butter, the exterior would melt away and burn before the center could heat through, and foie gras cooks similarly. By starting with everything at room temperature, the interior becomes perfectly cooked just as the exterior develops a golden brown crust.
NOTE To avoid overcrowding, cook the foie gras slices in two sauté pans.

Makes 4 portions

- Remove the foie gras from the refrigerator and cut into four 1½-inch-thick slices (they should weigh about 3 ounces each). Set aside at room temperature for 15 minutes. Meanwhile, combine the diced mango, shallot, thyme, sugar, rice wine vinegar, olive oil, chives, and salt and pepper in a small mixing bowl. Toss gently and reserve.
- Place hazelnuts in a small sauté pan and toast over high heat until lightly browned and fragrant, about 2 minutes.
- Crush the hazelnuts using a mortar and pestle or spice grinder. (Or place them on a cutting board, cover them with the bottom of a saucepan, and crush them by pressing down firmly.)
- Season the foie gras with salt and pepper.
- Place two pieces of foie gras in each of two unheated sauté pans.
- Set the sauté pans on the stovetop over high heat and cook the foie gras until golden brown, 2 to 3 minutes.
- Pour off any excess fat given off by the foie gras, gently flip each piece, and reduce heat to medium.
- Cook for another 2 to 3 minutes, remove from heat, and let foie gras pieces remain in pans for another minute.
- Transfer the foie gras to a plate lined with paper towels to absorb some of the excess fat.
- Place 1 spoonful of the mango salad in the center of four dinner plates.
- Arrange one piece foie gras on the top of each salad.
- Spoon Mango Vinaigrette in a circle around the salad and drizzle a bit over the foie gras.
- Garnish with crushed toasted hazelnuts, and serve.

MANGO VINAIGRETTE

1 cup ripe mango, cut into medium pieces

2 ounces (¼ cup) rice wine vinegar

1 ounce (2 tablespoons) pure olive oil

1 ounce (2 tablespoons) freshly squeezed orange juice

1 pinch togarashi (see note on page 24; cayenne pepper can be substituted)

1 pinch salt

1 pinch sugar

2 to 3 ounces (4 to 6 tablespoons) water, if needed

This vinaigrette is also wonderful on fish and shellfish. I like to serve it with Grilled Swordfish with Corn, Tomato, and Lime (page 22).

NOTE Mango Vinaigrette will keep for up to a week in your fridge.
ANOTHER NOTE Papaya or guava can be substituted for the mango.

Makes 1 cup

• Place all of the ingredients except the water in a blender and puree on high speed until smooth.
• If the puree seems too thick, thin it with a few drops of water and puree to incorporate.
• Keep adding water (a few drops at a time) until the puree has a saucelike consistency.
• Adjust the seasoning if needed. It should be both sweet and slightly tart.
• Reserve and serve at room temperature.

LOIN OF VEAL
WITH BLACK TRUMPET MUSHROOM RAGOUT

Veal and mushrooms. These ingredients are simple enough, and this is a down-to-earth preparation, but it is made elegant by focusing on product and technique. I've scaled this recipe for a tasting dinner. For entrée-sized portions you can double it and serve the veal on a bed of Robuchon Potatoes (page 134). A few spoonfuls of Truffle Vinaigrette (page 176) will add even more dimension.

Makes 4 tasting portions

- Preheat the oven to 300°F.
- Season the veal with salt and pepper.
- Heat the canola oil in an ovenproof sauté pan over medium heat.
- Add the veal and cook gently for 1 minute on each side. Do not brown.
- Add 1 pinch thyme and 1 teaspoon butter and continue cooking 1 more minute, basting several times with the melted butter and thyme.
- Place the pan in the oven and roast 16 to 18 minutes, or until medium. Baste and turn the veal over every 5 minutes or so as it cooks.
- Meanwhile, melt the remaining 1 teaspoon butter over high heat in a medium sauté pan. Add the shallot and cook for 1 minute.
- Add the mushrooms, season with salt and pepper, and add the remaining 1 pinch thyme.
- Add the vegetable stock and the juice of half the lemon to the mushrooms and cook until the liquid has reduced enough to just coat the mushrooms.
- Taste for seasoning and reserve until the veal is finished cooking.
- Remove veal from oven and let rest 5 minutes in a warm spot.
- Place one spoonful of the mushrooms in the center of each of four dinner plates.
- Drizzle the veal with the juice from the remaining lemon half.
- Arrange the veal loins on top of the mushrooms.
- Garnish with the chives, spoon the Truffle Vinaigrette on and around the veal, if desired, and serve.

4 4-ounce pieces of veal loin, 1-inch thick

Salt and pepper

2 ounces (¼ cup) canola oil

2 pinches fresh thyme leaves, chopped

2 teaspoons butter

1 shallot, minced

1½ cups black trumpet mushrooms, cleaned (fresh porcini or chanterelle are great substitutes)

2 ounces (¼ cup) Clear Vegetable Stock (page 214; chicken stock or water can be substituted)

Juice of 1 lemon

1 teaspoon finely sliced fresh chives

CHOCOLATE CINNAMON BONETS

INFUSED WITH BAY LEAF

FOR THE
BONET BASE

2½ cups whole milk

1 bay leaf

1 cinnamon stick

½ vanilla bean

1 teaspoon rum

6 tablespoons unsweetened cocoa

1⅓ cups sugar (⅔ cup for the steeped milk and ⅔ cup to be whisked with the yolks)

7 large egg yolks

1 pinch salt

FOR THE
CARAMEL

⅔ cup sugar

3 ounces (⅓ cup) water

1 teaspoon lemon juice

Whipped cream, for garnish

If you are like me and feel that making desserts is a daunting task, this is a recipe for you. It is a real showstopper, and I can't remember ever having it behave improperly. Serve garnished with freshly whipped cream.

Serves 6

FOR THE BONET

• Bring the milk, bay leaf, cinnamon stick, vanilla bean, and rum to a boil in a saucepan over high heat.
• Remove from heat, cover, and allow to steep for 1 hour.
• Remove the bay leaf, cinnamon stick, and vanilla bean.
• Add the cocoa and ⅔ cup sugar and whisk until frothy and well combined.
• Combine the egg yolks, the remaining sugar, and the salt in a mixing bowl and whisk until pale yellow and creamy.
• Reheat the milk mixture just to a boil, remove from heat, and slowly whisk in the yolks in a thin stream.
• Chill for 30 minutes.
• Preheat the oven to 325°F and coat six ramekins with nonstick spray.

FOR THE CARAMEL

• Combine the sugar, water, and lemon juice in a small sauce pot, place over high heat, and stir a few times to dissolve the sugar.
• Spray a ceramic pitcher with nonstick spray.
• Let mixture boil until the sugar caramelizes and turns dark brown.
• Immediately remove from heat and pour into the pitcher. Careful — caramelized sugar is very hot!
• Working quickly, pour enough caramel into each ramekin to coat the bottom and sides. Tilt each ramekin to help coat the sides and distribute caramel evenly.
• Fill each ramekin with the bonet mixture. With a spoon, remove any bubbles that form on the surface.
• Place the bonets in a large baking pan and carefully pour in enough hot water to come halfway up the sides of the ramekins.
• Cover the baking pan with aluminium foil and bake until custards are just set, about 1 hour.
• Allow to cool, and then refrigerate up to 2 days before serving.

TO SERVE

• Run a knife around the inside rim of the ramekins.
• Tap each ramekin on the work surface a few times to loosen the bonets.
• Place a dessert plate on top of each ramekin and then quickly invert.
• Carefully remove the ramekin. The bonet and the caramel will easily release from the ramekin.
• Serve with whipped cream.

SPRING

Sitting quietly, doing nothing

Spring comes, and the grass grows by itself

Eicho

SPRING TASTING MENU

Chilled Cucumber and Apple Soup with Curry

Roasted Halibut with Asparagus and Morels

Loin of Lamb with Quick Ratatouille and Spiced Vinaigrette

Lemon Sabayon Tarts

CHILLED CUCUMBER AND APPLE SOUP

WITH CURRY

2 Granny Smith apples, peeled, cored, and cut into 1-inch pieces

Juice of 1 lemon

4 English cucumbers, halved lengthwise and cut into 1-inch-wide pieces (do not peel)

¼ teaspoon curry powder

1 cup baby spinach, cleaned

6 cups Clear Vegetable Stock (page 214)

Salt and white pepper

A pinch or 2 of sugar, or to taste

4 ounces (½ cup) heavy cream

10 to 15 ice cubes

You can serve this soup from early spring on through to the first days of fall, and it comes together with very little fuss. I love chilled soups, especially soups as pleasantly tart and spicy as this one. If you'd like, garnish with cooked diced shrimp, lobster, or crabmeat.

NOTE Once the vegetables are cleaned and chopped, this soup will take you all of seven minutes. It really should be served as soon as it is pureed; it tends to oxidize and turn a rather unappealing shade of brown if it sits around for too long before you serve it. Yuk. So have all the ingredients ready to go, give them a whirl in the blender, and serve immediately.

ANOTHER NOTE If you have a standard 32-ounce blender, divide the ingredients in half and puree in two batches.

Makes 2 quarts of soup, plenty for 6 people

• Squeeze the lemon juice over the apples and toss to coat well. (This helps keep them from turning brown.)
• Divide the ingredients in half to make two batches.
• Puree each batch on high speed until very smooth, 2 to 3 minutes. (The ice cubes will dissolve and chill the soup.)
• Combine the batches, taste, adjust seasoning, and serve.

ROASTED HALIBUT
WITH ASPARAGUS AND MORELS

When asparagus and morels start turning up at the market, it is a sign that spring has truly arrived, and it is definitely cause for celebration. I can pass on many of the season's supposed delicacies — you can keep your rhubarb and your fiddlehead ferns — but I'll drop whatever menu plans I might have to create a meal around asparagus and morels.

Makes 4 tasting portions

- Preheat the oven to 300°F.
- Heat the canola oil in a large, ovenproof sauté pan over high heat for 1 to 2 minutes.
- Season the halibut with salt and pepper on one side only and place seasoned-side down in the pan.
- Gently shake the pan once or twice to make sure the fillets are not sticking, then cook undisturbed until you start to see golden brown edges on the bottom of the fish, 2 to 3 minutes.
- Lower the heat to medium, season the fillets with salt and pepper, and carefully flip to begin browning the other side.
- Add 1 pinch of thyme and 1 tablespoon butter, swirl the pan to combine, and cook 1 more minute, basting the fillets a few times with the oil and melted butter.
- Transfer the fillets to the oven and roast until done, 5 to 6 minutes.
- Meanwhile, melt the remaining butter with the olive oil in a medium sauté pan over high heat.
- Add the shallot and cook for 2 minutes.
- Add the morels and sauté for another 2 minutes.
- Stir in the asparagus and the vegetable stock and cook until the liquid has reduced enough to just coat the vegetables.
- Season with salt, pepper, and the remaining pinch of thyme.
- Squeeze the lemon half over the vegetables and remove from heat.
- Remove the halibut from the oven after it is just cooked through. Baste once more, and then squeeze a few drops of lemon juice over the fillets.
- Place a spoonful of the asparagus and morel mixture in the center of each of four dinner plates.
- Arrange the halibut on top of the vegetables.
- Spoon a tablespoon of Carrot Reduction around the vegetables, if desired, or drizzle with your best extra-virgin olive oil and another squeeze of lemon.

3 ounces (6 tablespoons) canola oil

4 4-ounce halibut fillets, skin removed (ask for pieces from the front or center of the fish, rather than the tail)

Salt and pepper

2 pinches fresh thyme leaves, chopped

2 tablespoons butter

1 ounce (2 tablespoons) extra-virgin olive oil, plus additional for drizzling over cooked fish

1 tablespoon minced shallot

½ cup fresh morels, cleaned and halved or quartered, depending on their size

6 asparagus spears, trimmed, blanched until just tender, and cut into thirds

2 ounces (¼ cup) Clear Vegetable Stock (page 214)

Juice of half a lemon

4 tablespoons Carrot Reduction, optional (page 176)

LOIN OF LAMB

WITH QUICK RATATOUILLE AND SPICED VINAIGRETTE

2 10-ounce boneless lamb loins

Salt and pepper

2 ounces (4 tablespoons) canola oil

2 pinches fresh thyme leaves, chopped

1 teaspoon butter

2 ounces (4 tablespoons) extra-virgin olive oil

½ clove garlic, thinly sliced

1 small shallot, cut into small dice

1 red pepper, cut into small dice

1 yellow pepper, cut into small dice

½ medium zucchini, cut into small dice

½ medium yellow squash, cut into small dice

¼ large eggplant, peeled and cut into small dice

1 plum tomato, quartered, seeded, and cut into small dice

Half a lemon

4 tablespoons Spiced Vinaigrette (page 219)

The vegetables in this dish do take some time to prepare, but once everything is cut up, the dish comes together quite easily. Don't be put off by all the dicing — a little patience and perseverance will go a long way here. I'm practically famous for my lack of fine-motor skills, so all I can say is "If I can learn to do it, so can you." Ideally, all of the vegetables should end up the same size, but don't fret if they do not come out this way on your first try. Nobody will die if the vegetables are not all perfectly uniform.

Makes 4 tasting portions

- Preheat the oven to 275°F.
- Season the lamb loin with salt and pepper.
- Heat the canola oil in a large, ovenproof sauté pan over medium heat. Add the lamb loins and cook gently, 1 minute per side. Do not allow the meat to brown.
- Add a pinch of thyme and the butter, swirl the pan to melt, and baste the lamb loins a few times with the oil and butter.
- Transfer the pan to the oven and roast until medium-rare, 15 to 20 minutes.
- Baste and turn the meat over every 5 minutes or so as it cooks.
- Remove the lamb from the oven and let it rest while you prepare the vegetables.
- In a large sauté pan, heat the olive oil and garlic over high heat. Cook for 1 to 2 minutes, until the garlic begins to turn brown.
- Add shallot and cook for 1 more minute.
- Add the remaining vegetables and sauté for another 3 minutes, until tender.
- Squeeze the lemon juice over the vegetables and season with salt and pepper.
- Place a spoonful of the vegetables in the center of each of four dinner plates.
- Slice each lamb loin into six even slices and fan three slices next to the vegetables on each plate.
- Drizzle spoonfuls of Spiced Vinaigrette on and around the lamb, and serve.

INDIVIDUAL LEMON SABAYON TARTS

I love the idea of individual desserts; no "He got a bigger piece than me!" complaints can be filed this way. Since there is already whipped cream in the sabayon, I don't think the tarts need another dollop on top. Instead, dust them with a little powdered sugar and garnish with fresh berries, if they are in season.

NOTE If you cannot find leaf gelatin, substitute 2 teaspoons powdered gelatin. Dissolve in 2 tablespoons warm water and allow to sit for 5 minutes before whisking into the lemon-egg mixture.

ANOTHER NOTE You will need six 3½-inch fluted tart molds for this recipe. If you like, you can use a 9-inch tart pan to make one large tart. Wrap any leftover pastry in plastic wrap and freeze for another occasion.

Makes 6 tarts

FOR THE TART SHELLS

- Combine dry ingredients with the butter in a mixer and blend on medium speed until the mixture starts to resemble sand.
- Add the remaining ingredients and mix on low speed until just incorporated. Refrigerate 15 to 30 minutes before rolling out.
- Preheat the oven to 325°F.
- Spray the tart pans with nonstick coating.
- Divide the dough into six pieces and form into small balls.
- On a lightly floured surface, roll each ball out into a circle, ⅛-inch thick and 6 to 7 inches in diameter.
- Transfer each pastry circle to a tart pan, press gently into place, and trim the edges.
- Place a piece of tin foil on top of each pastry, making sure it covers the dough completely.
- Fill each foil-lined tart pan with uncooked beans of any kind. (This is known as blind baking. I know it sounds ridiculous, but it keeps the pastry from shrinking while it bakes.)
- Bake the tart shells, beans and all, in the oven for 15 minutes.
- Let tart shells cool, then carefully remove the beans and foil. You can use the beans a second time for cooking pastries, but don't try to serve them for dinner.

FOR THE SABAYON

- Fill a small saucepan with 3 inches of water and place over high heat.
- Whisk the egg yolks in a large metal bowl for 3 minutes until pale golden and creamy.
- Whisk the sugar into the yolks and place the bowl over the pan of boiling water.

directions are continued on following page

FOR THE TART SHELLS

2⅓ cups all-purpose flour, sifted

⅓ cup granulated sugar

1 pinch salt

1 pinch baking powder

10 tablespoons butter, softened

1 egg

1 egg yolk

1 tablespoon heavy cream

FOR THE LEMON SABAYON

6 egg yolks

½ cup superfine sugar

3 ounces (6 tablespoons) fresh lemon juice

2½ cups heavy cream

4 sheets of gelatin, bloomed in ice water according to package directions (see note)

- Lower the heat to a simmer and cook 1 minute, whisking constantly.
- Begin adding the lemon juice in 2-tablespoon increments, whisking for 1 minute between additions.
- After all the lemon juice has been added, continue whisking until the mixture is rich, creamy, and thick, 5 to 7 minutes total cooking time.
- Remove from heat and taste for sweetness and acidity, adding more sugar or lemon juice, if desired. The egg mixture should be quite lemony and somewhat sweet. Set aside.
- Pour the heavy cream into a metal mixing bowl. Nest the mixing bowl in a larger bowl filled with ice, and whip the cream with an electric beater until stiff peaks form.
- When the egg mixture has cooled to room temperature, add the dissolved gelatin and whisk to incorporate.
- Gently fold the whipped cream into the egg mixture.
- Taste again for sweetness and acidity, and adjust accordingly.

TO SERVE
- Divide the sabayon between the cooled tart shells and refrigerate until set, about 2 hours. (Fill the tarts immediately after preparing the sabayon, otherwise it will become too firm.)
- Just before serving, dust tarts with powdered sugar and garnish with fresh berries, if desired. (This tart can be made up to 12 hours in advance, but it really is best when served the day it is made.)

Chapter 9

BASICS

Here are some basic recipes for items that are constantly called for in this book. I know that making your own stock may seem like a daunting task, but it really isn't all that difficult. Once you get all of your ingredients together, the stove does all the hard work. When finished, I suggest freezing the stocks in small containers so you have them at the ready whenever you get the urge to cook yourself a little something — these stock recipes produce something that tastes so much better than any canned item you are able to buy.

CLEAR VEGETABLE STOCK

Makes 4 quarts

2 large white onions, peeled

1 leek

2 large carrots, peeled

1 large bulb fennel

3 stalks celery

1 medium zucchini, peeled

1 medium yellow squash, unpeeled

4 quarts water

8 to 12 black peppercorns

1 bay leaf

1 orange, cut in half

- Roughly chop all of the vegetables into 2-inch pieces; precision is not important.
- Fill a large stockpot with the water, add the vegetables, and place over high heat.
- When the water comes to a boil, lower the heat to a simmer and add the peppercorns and bay leaf.
- Let simmer, uncovered, for 2 hours.
- Squeeze the orange into the stock, then add the two halves, skin and all.
- Turn the heat off and allow to steep for 15 minutes.
- Strain and chill. This stock freezes well; store in 8-, 16-, or 32-ounce plastic containers.

CHICKEN STOCK

Makes 2 quarts

6 pounds chicken bones, cut into 4- to 6-inch pieces (necks and backs are best)

2 cups white onion, peeled

1 cup celery

2 cups carrots, peeled

1 large leek, rinsed

4 quarts water

2 sprigs fresh thyme

8 to 12 peppercorns

- Roughly chop all of the vegetables into 2-inch pieces; precision is not important.
- Place all of the ingredients in a large stockpot and set over high heat.
- Bring to a boil, then reduce heat to maintain a slow simmer. Do not let the stock boil.
- Let the stock cook gently, uncovered, for 6 to 8 hours. Check frequently and skim off any impurities that come to the surface.
- Remove from the heat and strain twice through a fine-mesh strainer.
- Place strained stock in a clean sauce pot and return to high heat to bring the stock to a boil. Turn the heat down to maintain a light boil; reduce to 2 quarts.
- Strain again.
- Use immediately, or refrigerate for up to five days. Stock freezes well; store in 8-, 16-, or 32-ounce plastic containers.

RICH-ROASTED POULTRY STOCK

Makes 2 quarts

- Preheat the oven to 375°F.
- Place the chicken bones in a roasting pan and roast in the oven until dark golden brown, approximately 1 hour. Do not allow to burn.
- Heat the oil in a large stockpot over high heat.
- Roughly chop all of the vegetables into 2-inch pieces; precision is not important.
- Add the vegetables and cook, stirring only occasionally, until they begin to caramelize, 5 to 10 minutes.
- Add the V-8 Juice and red wine. Continue cooking over high heat for 5 minutes.
- Add the roasted bones and cover with water.
- Add the peppercorns and thyme sprigs.
- Bring to a boil, then reduce heat to maintain a slow simmer. Do not let the stock boil.
- Let the stock cook gently, uncovered, for 6 to 8 hours. Check frequently and skim any impurities that come to the surface.
- Strain twice through a fine-mesh strainer.
- Place strained stock in a clean sauce pot, return to high heat, and reduce to 2 quarts.
- Strain again.
- Use immediately, or refrigerate for up to five days. Stock freezes well; store in 8-, 16-, or 32-ounce plastic containers.

6 pounds chicken bones, cut into 4- to 6-inch pieces (necks and backs are best)

2 ounces (¼ cup) olive oil

2 cups white onion, peeled

1 cup celery

2 cups carrots, peeled

1 large leek, rinsed

5 ounces (½ cup plus 2 tablespoons) V-8 Juice

4 ounces (½ cup) red wine

4 quarts water

8 to 12 peppercorns

2 sprigs fresh thyme

VEAL STOCK

Makes 2 quarts

6 pounds veal bones, cut into 4- to 6-inch pieces (ask your butcher to do this for you)

2 ounces (¼ cup) olive oil

2 cups white onion, peeled

1 cup celery

2 cups carrots, peeled

1 large leek, cleaned

5 ounces (½ cup plus 2 tablespoons) V-8 Juice

2 tablespoons tomato paste

8 ounces (1 cup) red wine

5 quarts water

8 to 12 peppercorns

2 sprigs fresh thyme

- Preheat the oven to 375°F.
- Place the veal bones in a roasting pan and roast until dark golden brown, approximately 1 to 2 hours, depending on the size of the bones. Do not let the bones burn.
- Heat the oil in a large stockpot over high heat.
- Roughly chop all of the vegetables into 2-inch pieces; precision is not important.
- Add the vegetables to the stockpot and cook, stirring only occasionally, until they begin to caramelize, 5 to 10 minutes.
- Add the V-8 Juice, tomato paste, and red wine. Continue cooking over high heat for 5 minutes.
- Add the roasted bones and cover with the water.
- Add the peppercorns and thyme sprigs.
- Bring to a boil, then reduce heat to maintain a slow simmer. Do not let the stock boil.
- Let the stock cook gently for 12 to 14 hours, uncovered. Check frequently and skim any impurities that come to the surface.
- Strain twice through a fine-mesh strainer.
- Transfer to a clean stockpot, return to high heat, and reduce to 2 quarts.
- Strain again.
- Use immediately, or refrigerate for up to five days. Stock freezes well; store in 8-, 16-, or 32-ounce plastic containers.

PARSLEY OIL

Makes ¾ cup

1 cup fresh spinach, rinsed

3 ice cubes

2 bunches Italian parsley (leaves only)

6 ounces (¾ cup) canola or grapeseed oil

- Blanch the spinach in salted, boiling water. Shock in ice water and drain.
- Place the ice cubes in a high-speed blender.
- Place the blanched spinach in a kitchen towel and wring out the juice directly over the ice cubes in the blender. Let chill for 1 minute.
- Add the parsley and the oil and puree on high for 2 minutes, until smooth.
- Transfer the mixture to a chinois and strain over a bowl, letting the oil drip through for a full hour to extract the most flavor.
- The oil keeps its deep green color for only one to two days, so use quickly.

FISH STOCK

Makes 2 quarts

- Roughly chop all of the vegetables into 2-inch pieces; precision is not important.
- Place the fish bones, vegetables, and tomato paste in a large stockpot and cover with water.
- Bring to a boil over high heat, then lower heat to maintain a simmer. Do not let the stock boil.
- Add the thyme sprigs and peppercorns.
- Let the stock gently cook, uncovered, for 2 to 3 hours. Check frequently and skim off any impurities that come to the surface.
- Strain twice through a fine-mesh strainer.
- Transfer to a clean stockpot, return to high heat, and reduce to 2 quarts.
- Strain again.
- Use immediately, or refrigerate for up to three days. Stock freezes well; store in 8-, 16-, or 32-ounce plastic containers.

2 cups white onion, peeled

1 cup celery

2 cups carrots, peeled

1 large leek, rinsed

1 bulb fennel

6 pounds of clean, well-rinsed fish-bones, cut into 4- to 6-inch-pieces (call ahead to the fish store and have them put aside)

2 tablespoons tomato paste

5 quarts water

2 sprigs fresh thyme

8 to 12 black peppercorns

RED WINE SAUCE

Makes ½ cup

- Heat the oil in a small saucepan over high heat for 1 minute.
- Add the shallot, carrot, and celery and cook for 3 minutes, stirring occasionally.
- Add the red wine and simmer until it is reduced by half.
- Add the veal stock and reduce until ½ cup of liquid remains.
- Strain through a fine chinois into another container.
- Add the thyme and rosemary and let steep for 20 minutes
- Add salt and pepper to taste.
- Strain again through a fine chinois and reserve for serving. Can be made several days in advance and refrigerated or frozen.

2 tablespoons extra-virgin olive oil

1 shallot, cut to medium dice

1 medium carrot, cut into 1-inch pieces

1 celery stalk, cut into 1-inch pieces

½ cup red wine

3 cups Veal Stock (see facing page)

1 sprig fresh thyme

1 sprig fresh rosemary

Salt and pepper

DUCK CONFIT
Makes 10 duck legs

10 meaty duck legs

Salt and pepper

Several cups rendered duck fat (enough to cover; if you cannot find duck fat, substitute canola oil)

In a traditional confit, pieces of duck are marinated/cured overnight in a spice mixture, and every chef seems to have his or her own special blend. I prefer to use just salt and pepper, and I start the cooking process right away. I think salting the duck and leaving it for any length of time can draw too much moisture out of the bird and result in dry, chewy meat. Before refrigeration, the traditional salt cure was needed to preserve the duck over the winter. Since I only need the confit to keep a couple of weeks, I can get away with less salt.

Duck confit is an essential component of cassoulet, and you can also serve the legs on their own: Remove duck legs from the fat, scraping away most of the excess with your fingers. Sear gently on both sides in a nonstick skillet until heated through and the skin is golden brown. Accompany with roasted potatoes or the lentils from the Loin of Venison recipe (page 182), or let meat cool, remove from the bone, and serve tossed with frisée lettuce, sherry vinegar, and good olive oil.

NOTE Meat cooked in fat that is even barely boiling will become very tough, so never let the cooking fat reach a boil; the oil should have little to no movement.

- Generously season the duck legs with salt and pepper and let stand for 30 minutes.
- Preheat the oven to 250°F.
- Place the duck legs in a single layer in a deep, ovenproof pan. Ladle enough rendered duck fat into the pan to cover the legs by about an inch.
- Place the roasting pan in the oven and gently cook the legs for about 2½ hours, or until the meat starts to pull away from the bone. (When done, about 2½ inches of the leg bone will be exposed.) Do not let the fat boil.
- Remove the pan from the oven and allow the legs to cool in the fat.
- Duck Confit will keep for two weeks in the refrigerator, provided the legs are completely covered in fat.

SPICED VINAIGRETTE

Makes 1 cup

- Place the olive oil and curry powder in a small sauce pot and steep over very low heat for 30 minutes.
- Remove from heat, let cool, and then strain through a coffee filter into a small container. (This can be done up to 3 days in advance.)
- Simmer the balsamic vinegar in a small sauce pot over high heat until reduced to 2 ounces (¼ cup).
- Combine the coriander, cumin, and mustard seeds in a dry sauté pan and toast over high heat until lightly browned and fragrant, about 3 minutes.
- Let the seeds cool, then coarsely crack using a mortar and pestle or spice grinder. (Or place on a cutting board, cover with a sauce pot, and crush by pressing down firmly.)
- Combine the olive oil, vinegar, ground seeds, and the remaining ingredients in a small bowl, whisking gently just to combine. (The vinaigrette should appear "broken," with the oil and vinegar separated rather than emulsified.)
- Allow to rest 30 minutes for the flavors to develop.

4 ounces (½ cup) pure olive oil

¼ teaspoon curry powder

7 ounces (¾ cup plus 2 tablespoons) balsamic vinegar

¼ teaspoon coriander seed

¼ teaspoon cumin seed

½ teaspoon mustard seed

⅛ teaspoon togarashi (see page 24; cayenne pepper can be substituted)

1 tablespoon minced shallot

1 teaspoon finely sliced fresh chives

Salt and pepper, to taste

SPICY LEMON VINAIGRETTE

Makes 1 cup

NOTE Extra vinaigrette keeps for five days in the refrigerator and can be tossed with any assortment of lettuces for a quick salad.

- Combine all ingredients in a bowl and whisk well.

6 ounces (¾ cup) extra-virgin olive oil

1 shallot, minced

1 large pinch fresh thyme leaves, chopped

Juice and chopped zest of 1 lemon

2 tablespoons sherry vinegar

⅓ teaspoon mustard powder

¼ teaspoon togarashi (see page 24; cayenne pepper can be substituted)

Salt and pepper, to taste

INDEX

(Numbers in bold indicate the page with the most information about a dish or ingredient.)